# IN MY TIME OF DYING

How I Came Face-to-Face with
the Idea of an Afterlife

## SEBASTIAN JUNGER

SIMON & SCHUSTER
New York   London   Toronto   Sydney   New Delhi

100 YEARS
SIMON &
SCHUSTER

1230 Avenue of the Americas
New York, NY 10020

Copyright © 2024 by Sebastian Junger

All rights reserved, including the right to reproduce this book
or portions thereof in any form whatsoever. For information,
address Simon & Schuster Subsidiary Rights Department,
1230 Avenue of the Americas, New York, NY 10020.

First Simon & Schuster hardcover edition May 2024

SIMON & SCHUSTER and colophon are registered
trademarks of Simon & Schuster LLC

Simon & Schuster: Celebrating 100 Years of Publishing in 2024

For information about special discounts for bulk purchases,
please contact Simon & Schuster Special Sales at
1-866-506-1949 or business@simonandschuster.com.

The Simon & Schuster Speakers Bureau can bring authors to
your live event. For more information or to book an event, contact
the Simon & Schuster Speakers Bureau at 1-866-248-3049
or visit our website at www.simonspeakers.com.

Interior design by Lewelin Polanco

Manufactured in the United States of America

1  3  5  7  9  10  8  6  4  2

Library of Congress Cataloging-in-Publication Data has been applied for.

ISBN 978-1-6680-5083-5
ISBN 978-1-6680-5085-9 (ebook)

*This book is dedicated to my dear friends*
*John Falk and Tim Hetherington,*
*who set forth far too soon*

# Contents

# We've Been Expecting You

I had an Al Merrick Tri Fin and a brand-new 5-millimeter winter suit, and I squatted on the beach waxing my board and watching heavy January surf pound the outer bar. The sand was hard with ice and scattered with storm wrack—lobster traps, busted-up carpentry, buoys, nets, dead fish, and shrubs ripped out of the dunes on the storm tides. The temperature was in the twenties and a high-pressure system had scraped the world clear of clouds and delivered a stiff little northwest wind that held the peaks nicely and feathered them before they plunged forward. The waves were well over head high, which was nothing I hadn't surfed before, but that was in the summer; I had no idea that a winter swell broke very differently. There were clues, though: bottom sand getting sucked up the wave faces, turning them dirty beige, and trapped air rupturing out their back walls as they collapsed. It was late morning on a weekday in mid-January, and

I was the only person on the beach. I stood up and stowed the board under my arm and waded into the water.

I had neoprene boots and hood, but the water was weirdly heavy; even smaller waves packed a punch. A nor'easter had passed offshore a day earlier and was sending back huge, perfect swells that broke with so much force, they left the water boiling almost until the next wave came through. I waited until a set swept over the bar and then pushed off and started digging for the horizon, hoping to get outside before more waves came in. I was in deep water between the bars, but the big sets closed out everything.

I made it outside and sat my board facing the sun and feeling the ocean shift and roll beneath me. The beach was barren and stripped by winter storms and looked very far away. A few times I tried paddling into waves, but they jacked up and went concave so fast that I always pulled out, heart pounding. I didn't know that winter bars are steeper, which pitches waves forward more violently, and that cold water is denser and breaks with more force. The result is that winter waves are far more powerful and dangerous than the same-sized wave in the summer. And you can't hold your breath for nearly as long in cold water—twenty seconds, maybe thirty. The only way to avoid the power of a breaking wave is to get off your board and dive deep, but depending on the water temperature, you might not be able to hold your breath long enough for the turbulence to subside. I was thirty years old, I'd surfed this spot since I was eight, and it never crossed my mind that I could die here.

I had been out there half an hour when I saw a huge wave

starting to shoal outside of the bar. It darkened as it came, advancing with the slow determination of something designed to kill you. More peaks were lined up behind it like the ranks of an advancing army. If the waves were starting to steepen that far out, they were true monsters, and I didn't know whether to paddle like crazy and try to get over them before they broke or just stay put and take my beating. I stopped paddling and sat on my board to calm myself before they hit. On the lead wave came, towering, reaching, and finally detonating right in front of me—the worst possible place. I was beyond all human intervention. I took one last breath, slipped off my board, and dove for the bottom.

The force was so shocking that I caught myself thinking, *There must be some mistake.* My board leash snapped immediately. Vortices heaved me up, changed their mind, drove me down, somersaulted me, stripped off my hood, stuffed my wetsuit full of sand, and thrashed me with what felt like actual malice. I had no idea which way was up, which was a problem because I ran out of air almost immediately. Ordinarily, the hydraulics of even a large wave dissipate in a few seconds, but this was different—it went on and on. The wave wanted me and was going to keep thrashing me in the darkness until I finally gave up and breathed in.

What amazed me was how malevolent the whole thing seemed—*Me? Why do you want me?* I was young and had no idea the world killed people so casually. Oddly, I remembered that there was a pile of dirty dishes in my sink that someone was going to have to deal with. Files and notes for a book I hoped to write on my desk. Work clothes scattered across the floor. My parents lived a hundred miles away, and I was essentially camping out in their summer house to write my book. It had no insulation, and the baseboard heaters were so wasteful and expensive that I almost never used them. I lived in quilted canvas work clothes and slept in a wool hat and sweater. On very cold nights, my drinking water froze. Virtually nothing bothered me. And now all of that seemed to be over.

As I slammed back and forth in the cement mixer hydraulics, I realized that my "vision"—a circle of gray light where I'd have been looking if my eyes were open—was starting to close down. Meanwhile, I could feel my throat starting to gag, which I knew would culminate in one last forced breath. I'd never come close to drowning before, but somehow my body knew everything. It knew what all the signs meant, what it would be forced to do, and how this would end.

The circle of light was down to a pinprick and the gagging in my throat was almost beyond countering. My thoughts had degenerated into a desperate *no, no, no.* And then I felt the awful hydraulics slacken—not by much, but enough to sense the buoyancy of my wetsuit. *That* way was up; if I could hold on a little longer, I'd survive. The wetsuit was rising. I gave a few kicks. I rose more. The world started to get lighter. Everything was turning green. Everything was turning white. I was in the foam. I was in the air. I was in the world.

And then I saw one more wave coming—just as big, just as malevolent. I breathed out, breathed in, and went back down.

---

When I was in my late twenties, I worked as a climber for tree companies. It was well paid, but I was told that if I did it for any length of time, I'd get hurt. Which I did. I'd hang a line fifty feet into a tree or spike the trunk with climbing irons and take the tree down in sections with a chainsaw. Often limbs or sections of trunk had to be rigged and lowered so that they didn't damage the house or whatever was below. I could take a tree down in its own circumference. I could section out and lower every piece of a hundred-foot white pine so that it barely dented the lawn. I was terrified of heights but learned how to not look down; I just concentrated on what was in front of me and made sure my knots were tied. I was scared of falling but never of chainsaws, until I cut myself across the Achilles tendon while up in a medium-sized elm. After that I wasn't scared of chainsaws, exactly, but I was a whole lot more careful with them.

I used a braided nylon line that tested at 6,000 pounds. To hold myself in place so that I could work, I used a knot called a climber's hitch that slid up and down but locked as soon as I loosened my grip. The carabiners were rated at around the same strength as the rope. Mighty forces, in other words, were at work keeping me alive eighty feet in the air with a running chainsaw.

The existential charm of tree work is that your fate is entirely in your hands. The stakes are high—your life—but as with chess, there are no random events. All the information you need to survive is right in front of you, and if you don't, it's because you made a mistake. That is not true of driving or air travel or combat or even crossing the street on a walk light. Gravity, momentum, friction, and the dynamics of weight at the end of a line are all available to be understood and managed. I forgot to lock the carabiner on my climbing line; *dumb, dumb, dumb*. I topped out a tree and it came back on me; unforgivable. When the top comes back on you—a bad cut, a gust of wind—the first thing it does is pinch your chainsaw bar. You've got to roll out of the way while holding on to the saw, which is still running, so that it doesn't get set in motion when the top finally comes off. It's doable, but you don't want to have to.

Once, I got a call from a woman who said a huge red oak had come crashing down at the bottom of her yard. She said she was doing dishes when she heard a cracking sound and looked up in time to watch it fall. Not a breath of wind that day. The trunk had been entirely hollowed out by ants, and if I'd been working in the tree at that moment, I'd have died. That is the only tree I've ever encountered where my life would have been in fate's hands, though I do know a guy who roped into a limb that had a hidden rot pocket that broke under his weight. He dropped the first ten feet of a fall that would have killed him and then jerked to a stop when the limb got jammed into a crotch on the way down. I asked what he did after he finished bouncing, and he said he climbed back up into the crown of the tree and went back to work.

Everyone has a relationship with death whether they want one or not; refusing to think about death is its own kind of relationship. When we hear about another person's death, we are hearing a version of our own death as well, and the pity we feel is rooted in the hope that that kind of thing—the car accident, the drowning, the cancer—could never happen to us. It's an enormously helpful illusion. Some people take the illusion even further by deliberately taking risks, as if beating the odds over and over gives them a kind of agency. It doesn't, but it's an odd quirk of neurology that when we are fighting the hardest to stay alive, we are hardly thinking about death at all. We're too busy.

Dying is the most ordinary thing you will ever do but also the most radical. You will go from a living, conscious being to dust. Nothing in your life can possibly prepare you for such a transition. Like birth, dying has its own timetable and cannot be thwarted and so requires neither courage nor willingness, though both help enormously. Death annihilates us so completely that we might as well have not lived, but without death, the life we *did* live would be meaningless because it would never end. One of the core goals of life is survival; the other is meaning. In some ways, they are antithetical. Situations that have intense consequences are exceedingly meaningful—childbirth, combat, natural disasters—and safer situations are usually not. A round of golf is pleasant (or not) but has very little meaning because almost nothing is at stake. In that context, adrenaline junkies are actually "meaning junkies," and danger seekers are actually "consequence seekers." Because death is the ultimate consequence, it's the ultimate reality that gives us meaning.

At 11:35 p.m. on October 3, 2021, a sixty-six-year-old woman named Ruth Hamilton of Golden, British Columbia, was woken up by a loud bang: a meteorite the size of a "large man's fist" had crashed through her roof and come to a stop on the floral-print pillow next to her head. The meteor had been streaking through space for millions or billions of years. Its trajectory was non-random and mathematically predictable if you could know all the variables, which you couldn't. Unlike tree work, they're almost infinite. Hamilton's survival came down to where she happened to lay her head. She spent the rest of the night sipping tea in an armchair and staring at the rock in her bed.

Combat reproduces that randomness extremely well. One day, I was leaning against some sandbags at a small American outpost in Afghanistan, and I felt some sand flick into the side of my face. Bullets travel roughly twice the speed of sound, so they arrive at their target well before the gunshots that fired them. The outpost was usually attacked from over a quarter mile away, which takes sound waves more than a second to cover. After the sand hit my face, I just had time to think *What the hell was that?* before hearing the rattle and clatter of distant machinegun fire. I was almost hit by the first rounds of the first burst of an hour-long attack. Like Ruth Hamilton in British Columbia, a few inches closer and I would never have known anything.

A few days later, we came under fire while on a foot patrol. It was plunging fire from across the valley that was almost impossible to take cover from; I found myself trying to hide behind a mountain holly hardly thicker than my arm. Bits of leaves drifted down from bullets that were chopping through the foliage over our heads, and gouts of dust erupted around my feet: more randomness. I was in and out of combat for a year, and the randomness never stopped—I just couldn't let myself think about it.

Several years later, my friend and colleague from the Afghanistan deployment, British photographer Tim Hetherington, went off to cover the civil war in Libya. At the last moment, I had to pull out of the assignment, so Tim took a clandestine boat trip to the besieged city of Misrata on his own. He arrived in the morning and was in a firefight by noon. Two doomed enemy soldiers were trapped in a burning building dropping their last hand grenades down the stairwell. Tim went back to a journalist safe house a few miles from the front line and returned later in the afternoon, almost immediately getting hit by a single 81mm mortar from Gaddafi's troops. One fighter lost his legs. A British photographer staggered away holding his abdomen to keep his intestines in. An American photographer named Chris Hondros took a chunk of shrapnel through the back of his head that did not kill him instantly but rendered him brain dead and beyond hope. And Tim took a small piece of metal to his groin—small, but apparently big enough to sever an artery.

The dead and wounded were loaded into a pickup truck, and the driver raced for the Misrata hospital. Tim bled out in the back of the truck looking up at the blue Mediterranean sky. The last thing he said was "Please help me" to a Spanish journalist who was sitting next to him. Did Tim know he was dying? Was he scared? He had no pulse by the time they got him to the hospital. Nurses rushed him into the trauma bay and gave him chest compressions, but there was no bringing him back. Because of Tim's role documenting the war in Afghanistan, the US military made it clear that they would get his body out of Libya no matter what. Tim was buried in London on a fine spring day. The service was at the Church of the Immaculate Conception in Mayfair, and his closed casket rested on an ornate catafalque beneath the priest's dais. One by one, Tim's loved ones shuffled forward to pay their respects.

A few weeks after getting home from London, I found my-self inhabiting a very different world from the one I'd left—dull, monochromatic, without much optimism or love. Against all logic I convinced myself that Tim's death was my fault and that it should have been me and not him. Some days, I even caught myself thinking that *he* was the lucky one to have died; I was going to have to see my life through to the very end. Things unraveled quickly after that. My first marriage ended. My father died. The best man at my wedding rented a car, drove to a sporting goods store, bought a shotgun, and ended his life in a parking lot.

But the randomness that can kill you will also save you. One night I was in a crowded New York bar and glimpsed a woman who seemed inexplicably familiar. That was impossible—we'd never met—but I was overcome by the feeling I knew her. Later, she told me that she had experienced the same thing. We peered at each other in puzzlement and soon started talking. Her name was Barbara, she was a playwright and had a light Irish accent that came and went with the topic. Her father was fifty-three when she was born and had fought the entirety of World War Two on foot in Europe. He returned to become the mayor of his hometown and raise a family of twelve, of whom Barbara was the youngest.

We talked with a kind of shocked relief, as if we'd lost touch long ago and had finally run across each other again. Eventually we got married and had a little girl and then another little girl. We lived on the Lower East Side of Manhattan and in an old

house in the woods in Massachusetts. One day when my youngest daughter was two, I told her that I loved her and asked if she
knew what the word meant. "Yes, Daddy," she said. "Love means,
*stay here.*"

Indeed. But I still had one more wave to get through.

There is an irrefutable (and unprovable) thought experiment
that when people drown, they construct an elaborate fantasy of their future to insulate themselves from what is actually
happening. The subjective experience of time supposedly breaks
down so that they enjoy this fantasy as if it were just a continu-
ation of the life that came before. Years after I almost drowned,
the thought crossed my mind that maybe I was *still* drowning
but didn't know it. Maybe my anoxic brain was just conjuring a
fantasy that seemed to have taken place over decades but in fact
was lasting only minutes or seconds.

The second wave was huge but somehow lacked the power
of the first, and after a few seconds, I floated to the surface and
began slowly stroking for the beach. I staggered out of the shore
break and collapsed on the sand and lay staring at the sky. I was
more or less where my body would have wound up if I'd drowned.
How blue the sky; how white the clouds. *You almost never got to
see clouds again*, I thought. *You almost never got to see anything.*

I lay on the frozen sand imagining myself dead: arms askew,
mouth full of sand, eyes blank. Someone walking their dog might
see me in my wetsuit and mistake me for a dead seal. My car was
in the parking lot and my wallet was in the glove compartment;
it wouldn't take long for the police to match me to my driver's

license. The phone would ring at my parents' house and my mother would answer. At first, she wouldn't understand. Then she'd scream. Eventually she would call my father at work and he, too, would go from confusion to horror to shock.

The news would ripple out through the small group of people who loved me and the larger group of people who just knew me. My sister would fly home from England, where she lived, and she and my parents would let themselves into the unheated summer house to find the sink full of dishes and army blankets nailed over door openings to keep the heat in. A desk I'd built out of a sawhorse and a piece of plywood was piled with research on every topic I could think of related to death at sea: meteorology, oceanography, the physics of wave motion, ship stability, drowning. I was writing about a swordfishing boat that had gone down with six men off the Grand Banks in 1991 and wanted to reconstruct their last days and hours and minutes as closely as possible.

I didn't know any of the men, but through my research I'd gotten to know their siblings, their girlfriends, their mothers. The process eventually came to feel so intrusive and wrong that I started dreaming about them—that is to say, the men occasionally visited me while I slept. One dream was particularly vivid: I was walking along the beach where I surfed when I spotted them sitting in a circle in the sand. I hesitated because I was sure they were angry with me for writing the book, but they just waved me over to join them.

Don't worry, they seemed to be saying. We've been expecting you.

# WHAT

The pain in my abdomen arrived without fanfare one September morning when my eldest girl was two and a half and the household was busy with a rolling series of tasks that would never quite get done. The pain was a sudden burning below my sternum that made me stand up straight and push my fingers into my gut. It was different from any pain I'd ever known, and I inexplicably thought: *This is the kind of pain where you later find out you're going to die.* The pain came and went for months. It was both bearable and weirdly debilitating, sometimes making me sit down in a kind of sick heat. Like many people, I've ignored a lot of unpleasantness in my life—hernias, kidney stones, broken ribs, ruptured tendons, marathons, combat patrols, chainsaw wounds—and I ignored this as well.

My younger daughter was born a couple of months later, and the Covid epidemic began a couple of months after that. My eldest daughter, Xana, was not in school yet, so we were able to leave New York City and move to a remote property on Cape Cod. Our house was built in 1800 and sat at the end of a dead-end dirt road surrounded by pine forests owned by the federal government. Part of it was an organic farm run by friends who also lived on the property. We cut firewood and seasoned it and split it and chased coyotes and foxes from the chicken coops and traded food and cleared trees that came down across the roads when storms blew through.

The winter was mild, and spring was cold and endless, and June came with its heat and southwest winds that raised an afternoon chop on the bay and covered the puddles and windowsills with bright green pollen. Because of Covid, Xana knew no other children; the human race was mostly composed of my wife and me and the couples who lived on the farm and a family with two teenage girls up the road. One day Xana and I walked out to the paved road to make chalk drawings and then returned the following morning to see if they survived a rainstorm that had rattled through that night. No trace of her efforts remained.

"The rain wouldn't do that if it saw how beautiful they were," Xana said. *That's the problem*, I thought: we have no idea whether the universe even notices us, much less cares. Later, when I tried to understand why I ignored six months of abdominal pain, the only answer I could come up with was that I had fallen for an adult version of my daughter's hopes. *Surely the universe doesn't wipe out good people for no reason*, I thought. *Surely the universe doesn't wipe out the fathers of young children.*

Then very early one morning, just as details of the world were emerging outside the bedroom window, I was wrenched from sleep by a dream of my wife and daughters sobbing and holding each other while I hovered oddly over their heads, unable to communicate with them. I screamed and waved, but they had no idea I was there. I was somehow made to understand that I'd died and couldn't comfort them because I'd already crossed over; they were forever beyond my reach. Not only that, but I'd died because I hadn't taken my life seriously. *"You could have been doing anything—even playing chess—but instead you chose to die,"* was how a voice explained it to me. I'd been careless, and now it was too late.

I woke up engulfed in anguish and shame. A gray light was coming through the windows, and I could make out the faces of my wife and daughters next to me. We slept together on a large floor pad, and most nights, Xana was between Barbara and me. Six-month-old Angela was on her other side. I hadn't crossed over after all; I was still in bed with my family. I slid my arm under Xana, who rolled toward me instinctively in her sleep and put her head on my shoulder. I felt the interstellar emptiness of death slowly getting replaced by human warmth and touch. Eventually, children start providing reassurance to their parents rather than the other way around, and for me, that moment arrived one June morning at age fifty-eight, just as it was getting light.

My own father was born and raised in Europe but immigrated to the United States after the German Army invaded France, where he and his family were living. He was half

Jewish on his father's side, and though he rejected any kind of ethnic identity, he began using his Jewish middle name in America to flush out the bigots. My father, Miguel, arrived at the port of Baltimore at age eighteen on a Portuguese cork freighter named the *São Tomé*. He made his way through the arrivals hall and was interviewed by an immigration official who asked what he was going to do with his life. My father said that he wanted to be a physicist, to which the official said, "Well then, you must go to MIT, in Boston. My son is there, and it's the best school in the country."

My father had never heard of MIT but did know about Harvard, which was his preferred choice. And he would have gone there except that—according to him—the admissions director said his test scores were so high that Harvard would let him in even though they'd "reached their quota of Jews." My father nodded, walked out, and enrolled at MIT.

My father was a scientist who didn't believe in anything that he couldn't measure and test. (Which, as he'd point out, isn't actually belief.) He brought Enlightenment-era rationality to the benign superstitions of my mother, who adhered to a hopeful slew of Eastern wisdom: energies, chakras, past lives, and dead friends visiting in the form of owls or crows. When my mother got cancer in her fifties, she announced that she would treat it exclusively with macrobiotics and yoga. My father asked if there were any medical studies supporting the idea that uterine cancer could be cured through diet, and she angrily accused him of being "too rational"—in other words, not respecting her beliefs. He said he would leave the marriage if she didn't get treatment, and they settled on a compromise of surgery but no chemotherapy—which, to her surgeon's surprise, she survived.

We did not go to church, obviously, so rationality had to provide the kind of reassurance that spirituality often does. It was entirely through my father's eyes, then, that I understood my dream about dying. By his thinking, the dream was terrifying but obviously had no predictive value. How could it? Your body can't understand problems in any cognitive sense, which is what your mind would need to make sense of the information. They are two separate operating systems: one has thoughts, the other has sensations. Otherwise, we wouldn't need CT scans and MRIs to know what was wrong; we could just ask our bodies and tell the doctor what to fix.

Nevertheless, the dream unsettled me enough to tell Barbara about it. I was fifty-five when Xana was born, and I attributed the dream to my fear of dying while my children were young. By evening, the dream had passed from my mind, and we all went to bed around nine o'clock. The windows were open, and the June air poured in until the surrounding forest was part of our bedroom, our dreams, our sleep. The shrieks of fisher cats sometimes woke us up, or coyotes baying over a kill, or strange chatterings that I was never able to identify. I had no nightmares but was woken—again at dawn—by a burning in my abdomen. It was lower down than usual and had an intensity that was new. After a while it went away, and I went back to sleep.

The date was June 16, 2020. My body had been heading toward this day my whole life.

The dirt road that leads to our house is deeply tracked and crowded with young oak and locust and pitch pine. The clay substrate holds water so that huge puddles form when it rains hard; you might drive three or four car lengths with water above the rocker panel. The driveway is several hundred yards long and ends at a garage and former horse barn with a 1931 penny embedded in its concrete floor. Next to that is a small post-and-beam cedar shake house that was originally built by the Hopkins family, whose ancestors arrived on the *Mayflower* in 1620. After the Great Depression, the Hopkins family sold the property to a socialist writer named Waldo Frank, who had been in the thick of some of the most prominent struggles of the century: the peace protests of World War One, the American labor strikes and, later on, the Cuban revolution. Frank's autobiography includes a photograph of him being greeted on the tarmac by Fidel Castro, who is in combat fatigues and carrying a Belgium-made FAL assault rifle. For decades, radicals of all sorts—communists, artists, homosexuals, opium smokers—had come to the woods of Truro and the narrow laneways of Provincetown to avoid federal scrutiny and lead their subversive lives. Frank died in 1967, and I bought the property from his son in 2000.

The fire chief told me to clear the underbrush back from the driveway so that his trucks could get through in case there was an emergency, and eventually a friend and I took our chainsaws and cleared a buffer all the way to the road. We left the slash where it fell but eventually the vegetation grew back, and for years I'd been telling myself to clear the road again. There is almost no cell service at the house, and the landline is so old that a hard rain will short it out for days, so a passable road was particularly important. And for some reason, *that* morning I felt an overwhelming urgency to do the job.

I still had all my gear from my years as a climber for tree companies. I gassed my cruising saw and touched the chain up with a rattail and started down the driveway. It was unpleasant work in the heat with the mosquitos rising out of the puddles and locust thorns grabbing my pants and shirt, but by midafternoon it was done. I put the end of the bar on my boot toe and palmed the handle and looked back at my work. *Ringling Brothers could get in here if they had to*, I thought. The two teenage girls from up the road had come to babysit, which didn't happen often, so I could either go running or spend a rare afternoon with my wife. I walked back into the coolness of the house and suggested to Barbara that we take a few hours for ourselves. For some reason, I felt compelled to add, "It's such a beautiful day, and no one ever knows how many of these they have left."

Later, Barbara told me that what I'd said had briefly upset her because it suggested an attitude about life where you're constantly at risk of losing everything. But then she thought, *If he's right, I'll wish that this was how we spent our last day together* and agreed to take the rest of the afternoon off. None of this was normal: not the dream about dying, not the compulsion to clear the driveway, not the passing thought of mortality. Barbara whispered to one of the babysitters that we were leaving for a while, and we made sure the screen door didn't bang behind us as we slipped out of the house.

Waldo Frank had built a writing studio on the highest point on his property, and a trail led to it up a hill that was now covered in thick pine forests. When Frank built the studio, the hill was part of a great bearberry moorland that rolled southward from the Pamet River, and he would have been able to look up from his writing desk to see Cape Cod Bay and even the Plymouth headlands twenty miles away. The cabin had a curved roof like the hull of a lapstrake boat and a small chimney for a coal stove and a narrow plank bed. I pulled the door open, and we stepped into the cool, slightly rotted air of the old cabin. It was around five o'clock in the afternoon.

The human body has around ten pints of blood in it—or "units," as doctors prefer. Women tend to have less blood than men and children have less blood than adults, but in all cases, a healthy person can lose around 15 percent of their blood without much effect. (Women commonly lose that much in childbirth.) At around 30 percent blood loss, though—three to four units—the body starts to go into compensatory shock to protect its vital organs. The heart rate increases to make up for low blood pressure, breathing gets faster and shallower, and capillaries and small blood vessels constrict to keep blood where it's needed most, in the heart, lungs, and brain. If you push your fingertip into the skin of a healthy person, you will leave a white spot that refills with blood almost immediately. If you do the same to someone in compensatory shock, the white spot lingers, even if the person seems functional and clear-minded.

At 40 percent blood loss, the body starts to cross over into a state from which it cannot recover on its own. All organs need oxygen to function, including the heart, and if blood pressure drops too far, the heart can't beat fast enough to maintain sufficient blood pressure for survival. At that point, the person goes from compensatory to hemorrhagic shock and actively starts dying. He or she may start shaking convulsively and slip in and out of consciousness. The person will be hallucinatory and delusional; in fact, they may have no idea they are dying. They may try to joke with the doctors or ask them why they look so worried. The brain, heart, and vital organs are not getting enough oxygen and are beginning to shut down, which accelerates a process of acid toxicity triggered by the initial shock of blood loss. Acidosis can kill people even though they received enough blood to keep their heart beating.

A person can die in two or three minutes if a major artery is severed or can hang on for hours if the blood loss is slower, as it was for me. Either way, without a massive blood transfusion—often delivered straight to the jugular—the patient will die. Forty percent blood loss could be likened to the "death zone" on Mount Everest, at 26,000 feet, where there is roughly one third the oxygen of sea level. Climbers stuck in the death zone have the same survival rate as people who lose half their blood outside the hospital, which is to say, zero.

Barbara and I spent an hour or so in Waldo Frank's cabin. Insects vibrated in the afternoon heat, and birds flustered in the treetops. A hawk rose shrieking on an afternoon thermal. And in that desultory place of ordinariness and safety a streak of pain filled my abdomen. It came out of nowhere and was immediately the only thing I could think about. The pain was worse than indigestion but did not feel *dangerous*—just very strange. I changed position to see if it would go away, and it didn't, so I tried to stand up. The floor reeled away from me as if I were standing on the deck of a ship, and I sat back down.

"How strange," I said. "I've never felt anything like this in my life."

Now my wife had a problem; there was no way to call for help, and I outweighed her by fifty pounds. She would have to get me out of the woods and back to the house on her own. I put my right arm over her shoulders, and she hooked her left arm around my waist, and we tried walking. I remember thinking that we were only minutes into this, and I already couldn't keep my feet; that couldn't be a good sign. While we shuffled down the trail, I tried to rule out problems. Heart attack? Probably not; I had no pain in my chest and none of the risk factors. Stroke? Probably not, either, for the same reasons. My mother had had diverticulitis; could my intestines have ruptured? That didn't sound too bad; I'd probably have an operation and be out of the hospital in a few days.

My mind slid around like a car on ice; as much as I tried, I couldn't stay in my lane. Months later, I asked Barbara what I had been like. "You were mumbling," she said. "You were not reassuring me because you knew something was wrong. You said, *I'm going to need help*. Your feet were still moving forward but your torso was completely leaned on me."

We finally made it out of the woods to the driveway, and Barbara opened the passenger side of the car and helped me onto the seat. It was the first time since we had left the cabin that she could look directly at my face. "There was something about the way you looked at me without seeing me," she told me. "And that's when I ran. I didn't know if you were going to die while I was running into the house; I didn't want you to be alone for a second."

I have a memory of Barbara saying she was going to get a glass of water and leaving at a run. I did not like the fact that she was running because it meant she was worried. Barbara found the babysitters playing on the floor with Xana and Angela and signaled the older one to follow her into the kitchen. The girl got up, and Barbara quietly told her to call an ambulance. The dial tone on the landline was pure static because of the recent rains, so the babysitter walked outside to try to get a signal with her cell phone.

Meanwhile, Barbara filled a glass and ran back outside. She started massaging my hands and telling me to try to stay with her. "You were slurring your words," she said. "You thought you were talking, but you weren't making sense." I was cycling in and out of consciousness, and Barbara was afraid that eventually I'd slip away and not come back. I remember the babysitter walking figure eights in front of the garage, trying to hook a signal. I caught her eye and saw how scared she looked, which triggered a flash of guilt. Xana ran out of the house to see what was going on and was scooped up just in time by the younger sister, who was fourteen.

My abdomen seemed to be simply made of pain and nothing else, which might have kept bringing me back to consciousness. It was around then that the sky began to turn electric white. The whiteness burned out the treetops and then the house and then the driveway and finally my wife's face. I told her I was going blind, and after that, I don't remember much. At some point Barbara said that the ambulance was coming, and after a while I heard sirens in the distance. There were words spoken by Barbara and then sirens again—louder now—and more pain and finally words spoken by a man. The face of a paramedic appeared where my wife's face had been.

"So, you don't feel well?"

In fact, I was feeling a little better; my vision had returned, and my mind had suddenly reengaged, as if someone had released a clutch and put me back in gear. No one realized I'd gone into compensatory shock. I wasn't even sure I needed to go to the hospital; if it weren't for the pain in my abdomen, I probably wouldn't have. The paramedics suggested drinking water in the shade—it was a hot day, they pointed out—and calling back if I didn't feel better.

Barbara said, "A few minutes ago he was going blind and passing out. He's going to the hospital."

I was clearheaded enough to remember the renowned statistic that married men live longer than unmarried men. *Surely this was one of the reasons*, I thought. The paramedics must have been through this dynamic many times before because they made a deal with me: if I could stand without assistance, I could stay home. It seemed like a low bar to clear, so I swung my legs over the side of the car seat, stood up, and promptly felt my knees go out. Even though I was feeling better, my blood pressure had tanked, and I could no longer stand up. The paramedics laid me on a stretcher and loaded me into the ambulance.

I watched the treetops of my driveway recede out the rear window. The paramedic who was with me in the back said his name was Joe. He put an IV line into my arm because my blood pressure was low and he assumed I was dehydrated, and the ambulance jolted off down my dirt road. It picked up speed when we hit pavement, and a few minutes later, the sirens came on and I felt us accelerate onto Route 6. From there it was nearly an hour to the hospital; our town has the second-longest emergency transport in the state.

Barbara still had no signal on her cell but was able to text. She sent a message to Uli, one of the young men on the farm, and told him there was an emergency and to come as fast as he could. He and Barbara sat on the kitchen floor keeping the girls distracted while the babysitters went home to pack overnight bags. She said to Uli, "I know this sounds dramatic, but I don't feel good about this."

"Oh no, it's not like that," Uli said. "He's going to be okay."

Barbara wasn't crying, but she was shaking uncontrollably. Should she have driven out to the highway and called the ambulance from there? Should she have run for help from the cabin rather than walking slowly with me? Were those ten minutes going to be the difference between me living and dying? Barbara was also very aware of having young children who had to be taken care of. Their needs came even before mine. "So, I just started gathering the forces," she told me later. "As long as the girls were safe, I knew I could go to you."

Back in the ambulance, I was worried I wasn't getting fluids fast enough and asked Joe to squeeze the IV bag, which I'd seen combat medics do in Afghanistan. I also asked for a second IV bag, to be safe. He said that wasn't necessary; the point is just to keep your systolic pressure at 80 or so, which is the minimum level for consciousness. Joe later said that he had ruled out abdominal hemorrhage because the heart rate generally shoots up to compensate for blood loss—often over 100 beats a minute—and my rate was practically normal. Young or athletic people have efficient hearts, though, that can maintain blood pressure without racing. "Younger people are famous for looking pretty good and then just falling off the cliff," the head of the emergency department in Hyannis told me. "They go from looking okay to dead. Good elasticity in your arteries, a strong heart . . . all those things are good. But when you get to the point where you can't maintain anymore, you're really far gone."

I certainly wasn't young, but a lifetime of running and working and moving had given me a vascular system that could mask the blood loss. I was bleeding out, and my heart rate had barely budged. I found my cell phone in my pocket and called my wife to tell her I was okay. She put Xana on, who told me that she loved me to the moon and back. I hung up without giving that the thought it deserved.

Halfway to the hospital, a spasm shot through me that lifted my body off the stretcher. It felt like hot lava had been injected into me. A few minutes later I lost control of my bowels and a foul-smelling liquid left me, mostly blood. That didn't seem good, but Joe wasn't worried. The obvious diagnosis was now something intestinal, he said, and my vital signs were still close to normal. I had an EMS priority of 2, which meant I'd been assessed as having something *potentially* serious but not immediately life-threatening. The emergency department at the hospital was barely tracking my arrival.

Joe could not have known this, but I was essentially a human hourglass, probably losing a unit of blood every ten or fifteen minutes. Both my vision and my bowels had failed in the past half hour, and for what it was worth, I'd seen both happen to badly wounded soldiers in Hollywood war movies, and it didn't seem like a good sign. I tried to figure out whether I was in danger or not by how the driver was handling the ambulance, but it was impossible to know. He seemed to be hitting the siren faster in traffic and accelerating with more intensity, but I no longer trusted my mind with information. I was just coherent enough to know that I wasn't entirely coherent.

We turned off the highway, which meant we had five or ten minutes to go, and then suddenly, we were in an underground loading bay, which made me think I must have lost consciousness for a while. The ambulance stopped, the doors opened, and an array of people in masks and scrubs appeared before me. I was alarmed by how many there were—was I in more danger than I realized?—and for some reason, I asked if I was in purgatory.

I was trying to be funny, but no one laughed. "No, because I'm here, and I'm pretty sure I'm going straight to hell," one of them finally said.

And then I was under bright lights, and a lot started happening very fast.

D r. Craig Cornwall, head of the emergency department at Cape Cod Hospital, Hyannis:

"Steve Kohler and I were working on the same team, and we basically alternate patients. We knew a belly pain was coming in and we knew . . . something was a bit amiss, but we didn't get the vibe that things were catastrophic. We were sitting at our desks, and we saw you go by and I said, *Oh, that doesn't look good.* You were gray. Minimally interactive. There is a certain look people have when they don't have much blood in their body, and you had that look. We don't care so much *what's* going on; we care what *class* of something is going on. And you had a vascular catastrophe of some sort."

The emergency department is a big bright room with desks and workstations in the center and exam rooms and trauma bays around the periphery. A trauma bay is large enough for seven or eight people at once—doctors, surgeons, nurses, anesthesiologists, radiologists—as well as supplemental oxygen, crash carts, and a vital-signs monitor. Dr. Cornwall and Dr. Kohler work near the ambulance entrance so they can watch new patients arrive, and when I went by, they glanced at each other, and Kohler jumped up to attend to me. "You looked like shit," he later told me. "Your blood pressure was sixty-eight. You were a 'zebra'—something we never see. I actually thought it was your aorta."

The aorta takes all the blood pumped by the heart—as much as a gallon and a half a minute—and distributes it throughout the body. The ascending aorta distributes blood to the chest and head and then continues as the descending aorta, which distributes blood to the abdomen and legs. The abdominal aorta is the width of a garden hose and under enormous pressure every time the heart contracts. If there is a weak spot in the garden hose, it will start to balloon outward in an abdominal aortic aneurysm— a "Triple A," as it's known. This ballooning can take decades and is often without pain or other symptoms. Most Triple As are diagnosed postmortem, if at all. Three percent of older Americans have aortic aneurysms that are at risk of rupture, and for those who experience a rupture, only about 10 percent make it to the hospital alive. Of those, almost half die in surgery.

So, when Dr. Kohler thought my aorta had ruptured, he knew he was dealing with someone who had a fifty-fifty chance of dying no matter what they did. It had taken me an hour and a half to get to the hospital, my blood pressure was ten points below the minimum for consciousness, and my hemoglobin levels were in the toilet. Hemoglobin carries oxygen from the lungs to the rest of the body; without enough of it, you lose consciousness and die. Periods of unconsciousness are known to be predictive of death with Triple As, and I'd been drifting in and out of reality almost from the beginning.

But I was still clear-minded enough to remember my home number and give it to Dr. Kohler. He dialed it, but at the other end, Barbara was hearing a ring, picking up the receiver, and just getting static. The lines were shorting out from the recent rains. Kohler eventually tried her cell phone, which worked. "Don't worry, we are going to take care of your husband," he told her. "But you should come."

Doctors often try to get family members to come in if they think the patient will die, because seeing a trauma team desperately trying to save their loved one is enormously comforting later on. That is particularly true for parents. Barbara told Kohler that the ambulance crew had said Covid restrictions would keep her from going inside the building, but he overrode that.

"I wouldn't drive a hundred miles an hour," he said to Barbara, "but if it were my wife, I would go as fast as I could."

Dr. Kohler has straight white hair tied in a ponytail and a lithe, fit build from competing in triathlons. He has a resting pulse in the 40s, which makes him a perfect candidate for masking catastrophic hemorrhage with a steady, unremarkable heart rate. Many years earlier, his wife had almost died of postpartum hemorrhage. Pregnancy and complications from childbirth are a leading cause of death for young women worldwide; if the woman has any unknown aneurysms, they can easily rupture during birth, often filling the uterus with blood. It's harder to bleed into a small, packed area than a large wide-open one, and the uterus is one of the most open spaces in the body. Kohler's wife started feeling light-headed after the birth and crashed right in front of him. "I got up to put an IV in her and *I* was getting light-headed," he said. "She goes into the OR and her blood pressure is like forty-five or fifty, even on a pressor agent. She basically bled out her entire body's blood supply. They did an emergency hysterectomy and she survived."

When Dr. Kohler rushed into the trauma bay and was told I had abdominal pain, low blood pressure, pallor, and had been in and out of consciousness, he knew that a massive abdominal hemorrhage was one of the few things that checked all those boxes. Maybe I had a bleeding ulcer, maybe I had a ruptured aorta, maybe I had a tumor that had finally eaten through an artery wall, but the first thing they had to do was find the bleed and stop it. If I'd been shot or stabbed, they would have known where to start looking, but internal hemorrhage can be almost anywhere, which makes it particularly deadly.

"You were now the sickest person in the hospital," Dr. Cornwall said. "We needed to mobilize the CT scan immediately."

I heard Dr. Kohler tell a nurse to take me to radiology "as fast as possible without actually running," and then hallways started going by and double doors started opening. By then I'd fully transitioned to end-stage hemorrhagic shock and my body was shaking convulsively on the gurney, its last attempt to stay alive. I felt myself getting lifted from the gurney onto a CT scanner—the "donut," as it's known—and could feel my body rattling against the shuttle board. I was very cold and in extraordinary pain. A nurse put a heated blanket on my body, which felt incredible, and led me through some breathing exercises. I remember thinking that these must be the breathing exercises that women use during childbirth, and I was amazed how well they worked. I was not sedated because my vital signs were already catastrophically low; suppressing them further with pain medication could kill me.

The reason for the convulsive shaking that had taken over my body was *hypothermia*—low body temperature. People with hypothermia slur their words, fail to make sense, can't comprehend what is happening, and are prone to hallucinations. I was doing all those things. In end-stage hypothermia, the dying person may take off their clothes—"paradoxical undressing"—or curl up in a small, dark place, like a closet or under a bed. "Terminal burrowing," as it is called, is thought to be initiated by a very primitive part of the brain associated with hibernating behavior in other animals.

Low blood oxygen from hemorrhage is indistinguishable from low blood oxygen from deep cold. The body starts expending huge amounts of metabolic energy trying to stay warm— burning the furniture because it's out of firewood, as it were. In this case, the furniture is glucose, which is stored in the body's cells. Burning glucose instead of oxygen is a desperate short-term measure because it produces lactic acid, which in turn impairs heart function. As heart function declines, the body gets less blood and sinks further into hypothermia, which lowers oxygen levels and clotting factors in the blood even more. Low clotting factors quickly culminate in *coagulopathy*, where the blood can't clot at all.

This feedback loop is known as the "trauma triad of death." You can dump as much blood as you want into a person, but once the coagulopathy cascade has begun, it's hard to stop. Ironically, the more saline you give a person before giving them actual blood, the more you dilute the clotting factors and the more danger they are in. Had Joe given me another IV bag in the ambulance, as I'd asked, my odds of entering the trauma triad of death would have gone up to 40 percent. Around one quarter of people who die of blood loss in the hospital have plenty of blood in their veins. They die of coagulopathy.

While radiology was trying to pinpoint the source of the bleeding, Dr. Kohler called a "code crimson," which mobilized the blood assets in the hospital and diverted enough staff to administer them. It was the first time the summer interns had heard that call. I initially received nine units of blood in total, which meant I'd probably lost two thirds of the blood in my body. Blood was the only thing that could save my life, but the more units you need, the more likely you are to die, and nine units was getting close to the upper end of the scale. A particular sequence of blood products must be used with people who are bleeding out—a "massive transfusion protocol"—and the delivery and verification of these products requires a very intense choreography. Bags of blood are easy to mix up during an emergency, and giving someone the wrong blood type can kill them.

The CT scan revealed a huge pool of blood in my abdomen and active bleeding around the pancreas. The doctors had a crucial choice. They could stabilize me with a transfusion and repair the rupture in the interventional radiology suite, where doctors use a fluoroscope to guide a catheter through your venous system, or they could open up my abdomen in surgery and try to find the rupture before I bled out. You must be "hemodynamically stable" to go to the IR suite, because if you code in IR, they have to rush you back into surgery to save your life. There, they can intubate you, transfuse you, defibrillate you, or split your chest open to massage your heart. But once the doctors open you up, they're elbow-deep in your abdomen and there is no going back. It's the civilian equivalent of combat surgery.

Furthermore, the clock was ticking. Once you open the abdomen, you lose any back pressure—*tamponade*—that may have been slowing down the blood loss, and blood can literally erupt from your abdominal cavity. During the Iraq War, the US military developed a technique where they opened the abdomen, quickly packed it with gauze to maintain tamponade, and then went quadrant by quadrant—moving organs aside, suctioning blood out—to find the source of the bleeding. But "emergency laparotomy," as it's called, is touch and go in the best of circumstances. Your odds of surviving are as low as 40 percent, depending on the trauma.

At some point, a young nurse appeared over me and whispered, "You didn't hear it from me, but it's not your aorta." I had no idea what she was talking about—wasn't I in for belly pain?—but she seemed excited about it, so I thanked her. Later I realized that, in her mind, she was giving me the good news that I had a chance of surviving. I must have lost consciousness after that, because my next memory was a new face peering over me back in the trauma bay: a young doctor named Spencer Wilson. He had been called in from surgery by Dr. Kohler to put a transfusion line into my neck, which freed Kohler to start coordinating other assets he would need: blood bank, interventional radiology suite, vascular surgeon. Dr. Wilson asked permission to put a large-gauge line into my jugular vein, which sounded painful and unnecessary. *Why would they need to do that?*, I wondered. I already had IV lines in both arms. "You mean, in case there's an emergency?" I asked.

"This *is* the emergency," Wilson said and started readying something called a Cordis line, which is used during massive transfusions. On some level I knew something was seriously wrong, but my brain wasn't working well enough to understand that I was dying. I didn't have any grand thoughts about mortality or life; I didn't even think about my family. I had all the introspection of a gut-shot coyote. Dr. Wilson reappeared above me upside down and put a transparent plastic sheet over my face to keep the area sterile. Then he pushed down hard on the right side of my neck to image my jugular with an ultrasound probe so that he could slide a needle into it.

While Dr. Wilson inserted the needle, he kept tugging at the plunger until he flashed blood in the syringe. That told him he was in my jugular. Then he slid a wire through a hole in the needle into my vein, pulled the needle out, slid a plastic dilator over the wire, pulled the wire out, and inserted a Cordis catheter. With a scalpel he cut into my neck and then sutured the line in so that it couldn't move. All of this can be perilous. The needle can rupture the vein, air can enter the bloodstream, or Dr. Wilson could lose his grip on the wire and allow it to get sucked into my jugular. Then—along with everything else—they would have to open another entry point in my groin and go fishing for the wire inside my vascular system.

During a massive transfusion protocol, trauma nurses sequence the blood products and call them out, and a doctor inspects them and signs for each one before it gets hooked up to the lumen, which leads to the jugular. For every blood packet, Dr. Wilson had to sign a document that read, "I believe this patient's life will be in jeopardy without an emergency transfusion, and therefore accept responsibility for adverse patient reaction." There generally isn't time to test for blood compatibility when someone is bleeding out, so doctors will use the universal blood type, O negative, and hope for the best. I somehow remembered that in Afghanistan I'd written "O+" on my helmet, and I told them that. Kohler ordered three packets of un-crossmatched O positive red blood cells to be delivered by rapid infuser into my jugular.

Blood is divided into three main components of red blood cells, plasma, and platelets so that it can be stored and shipped more easily and used more efficiently. Blood fractionation, as it's called, mostly solves a supply problem rather than a medical problem. In fact, a military study from US combat operations in Iraq and Afghanistan between 2004 and 2007 found that transfusions of fresh whole blood into badly wounded soldiers significantly increased their survival rates. Hospitals are forced to play a kind of shell game with limited blood supplies, though; some of the blood I was given was due to expire within hours. Severe trauma is rare, but if multiple trauma patients hit a hospital at the same time, there might not be enough blood to go around. During disasters such as earthquakes or terror attacks, blood supplies run out and doctors are forced to make decisions about who is likely to survive and who isn't. The death rate for the kind of hemorrhage I had is 50 percent to 70 percent. During a mass casualty event with limited blood resources, I might just be sedated and allowed to die.

Dr. Wilson seemed to be taking a long time getting the Cordis line into my jugular, and while he worked, I became aware of a dark pit below me and to my left. The pit was the purest black and so infinitely deep that it had no real depth at all. I was on the gurney, with Dr. Wilson upside down above my head and the other nurses and doctors seemingly all clustered on my right side. Meanwhile, there was nothing on my left side except the blackness that I was getting drawn into. It exerted a pull that was slow but unanswerable, and I knew that if I went into the hole, I was never coming back.

I later asked Dr. Kohler what was going on with me, medically, at that point. He said, "You were getting ready to buy the farm." (The term is thought to come from the families of dead soldiers, who used government death benefits to pay off property debt.) Dr. Cornwall, his supervisor, estimated that I was ten to fifteen minutes away from cardiac arrest and death. Wilson was still working on my neck, and I was feeling myself getting pulled more and more sternly into the darkness. And just when it seemed unavoidable, I became aware of something else: My father. He'd been dead eight years, but there he was, not so much floating as simply existing above me and slightly to my left. Everything that had to do with life was on the right side of my body and everything that had to do with this scary new place was on my left. My father exuded reassurance and seemed to be inviting me to go with him. "It's okay, there's nothing to be scared of," he seemed to be saying. "Don't fight it. I'll take care of you."

I was enormously confused by his presence. My father had died at eighty-nine, and I loved him, but he had no business being here. Because I didn't know I was dying, his invitation to join him seemed grotesque. He was dead, I was alive, and I wanted nothing to do with him—in fact, I wanted nothing to do with the entire left side of the room. And I didn't understand why Dr. Wilson was taking so long to finish his work.

"Doctor, you got to hurry," I told him. "You're losing me. I'm going right now."

And that was the last thing I remembered for a very long time.

*It was already snowing when I left the hotel, I remember, and I dropped my bag with the desk clerk and told him I'd be back in a couple of days. I was twenty years old and had cigarettes and a few hundred dollars and an American passport in my pocket and an old leather coat that looked cool but held no warmth at all. Students were huddled in cafés and bars, and old women in black moved one by one over the cobble, married now to God, as the saying goes. I made my way past the university and through the Old Town and across the Tormes to the rail station.*

*There were fast trains east to Madrid-Atocha and Ávila and north to Valladolid, but I was headed out on a small line into the mountains. My father had told me that the mountains south of Salamanca still had bears and wolves, and I wanted to see such a place. Republicans had fought the fascists from these mountains and then from the Escorial and finally in the streets of Madrid. The mountains south of Salamanca were called the Sierra de Gredos. I studied a road map and picked a town in the direction of Béjar and bought a ticket.*

*The local trains were unheated and rode like buckboards. I bought a coffee and sherry across from the station and watched the snow come down and climbed into my train when the engines started up. For a while, I was the only person in the car. I watched the fields go by and the small towns and the low hills. It snowed harder as we climbed, and then there were roadcuts and pine forests draped in snow and frozen little hamlets with no people at all.*

*Finally, my town came. I don't remember the name, but it was somewhere past Béjar, surrounded by fields and forests and the low stern peaks of the De Gredos. I was the only person to get off the train. Steel creaked against steel and the wheels gathered speed and then I was alone. I headed for the center of town, walking in the road because the right-of-way was under two feet of snow, and I asked the first man I saw where I could find a hotel.*

*"No hay hoteles," he said. I asked if there was a restaurant, but he shook his head. "Hay un café," he said, chopping his hand in the air in the direction of town. "Todo derecho. Pero, cuidado con los militares."*

*Franco had been dead since '75, but his mourners had raised the fascist salute at his funeral and the military and police still had a long way to go. Now I was walking into town with snow falling and dusk quickly taking over the world. I headed for a group of young men smoking under a lamplight and they hardly made way for me when I tried to step past them into the bar. There were more of them inside, dressed in military fatigues and smoking cigarettes and drinking narrow cañas of beer. They looked at me and the bartender looked at me and I turned and walked back out.*

*It was almost dark and already very cold. I walked back the way I'd come and continued until I was beyond all the houses and surrounded by fields. At the edge of the fields were pine woods and then, much farther, the mountains. The pines were bowed over like cowled pilgrims on the Camino. Pine trees are thick with dead branches in their understory, and to the extent that I had a plan, it was to cross the field into the woods and collect enough deadwood to get a solid flame going in the snow. Then I would light a cigarette and smoke it while considering my situation and eventually head back out to collect more wood. Snow always reflects a little light, and I would continue collecting wood and feeding the fire until dawn. I had enough cigarettes to last the night, which was almost as comforting as the thought of the fire. I'd spent plenty of nights in front of a fire and knew that if I kept it fed, I'd be okay. In the morning I'd get a train back to Salamanca.*

*I walked along, trying to pick my spot to leave the road and head for the woods. Car headlights swept over me from the direction of town, and I got ready to step off into the snow to let them pass. I could hear the car coming up behind me, and my giant shadow lurched and heaved in the headlights. Just as I was getting ready to step into the snow, I could hear the tires slow down on the pavement. That's not good, I thought. Now the car was stopping. Now a man was leaning across the seat to crank the passenger window down.*

*"¿Dónde vas?" he asked. He was in his fifties.*

*"Salamanca."*

*"Yo también."*

*I hesitated and then opened the car door and got in. From inside, night looked like it had already seized the world.*

*"Que estás haciendo aquí?" he said.*

*I told the man about the bears and the wolves, and how the Republicans had fought the fascists from these mountains and then from the Escorial. I told him that my father had lived in Madrid as a little boy but had to flee with his family when Franco came in.*

*The man shook his head. "No hay lobos todavía," he said. "Ni osos."*

*There are no wolves anymore, nor bears. He didn't mention the fascists. He easily could have been one, but of course they're not all bad people, I thought. My father's family had close friends who were fascists. It took a couple of hours to get back to Salamanca, and the man dropped me near the university. The snow had stopped, and young people were walking in couples and groups through the odd angles of the streets, laughing and chatting. I felt like I'd come back from the dead and didn't even feel entirely visible. I walked to a bar that I knew and ordered a caña and sat down and lit a cigarette. The students around me were my age and seemed very happy to be there at that moment in their young lives, with their friends around them and the evening so beautiful in the new snow. I was told it snowed all the time in the mountains but rarely down here on the plains.*

*I felt like I was half there and half crouched under a pine tree feeding a fire. Such a small bit of luck had kept that from happening that it almost seemed as if both were happening at the same time and that I would have to continue as two different people. Was there another universe where I spent the night under the tree and returned to make other choices and lead an entirely different life? Was there another universe where I froze to death?*

*When I got home, I told my father the wolves and bears were*

*gone, but that the mountains seemed as wild as ever. "At least you
went," he said. "That's the real point."*

My father was an odd choice for a deathbed visitation, and
I'm pretty sure he would have agreed. His particular kind
of intelligence was so literal that he could easily be mistaken for
simpleminded. With bright blue eyes and a handsome Mediterranean face, he had the appearance of someone who would
be completely at ease in the human world, but he often entered
it like a scuba diver with forty-five minutes of air and a weight
belt to keep himself down. That was particularly true around my
mother's friends, who were mostly artists and yogis and macrobiotics. He had scripts for common conversations and when he
ran out of those, he just closed his eyes and started talking about
the ancient Greeks.

And this was the man who had appeared above me as I was
dying. He was not so much a vision as a mass of energy con-
figured in a deeply familiar way as my father. I hesitate to even
describe him as "energy" because it was a word he hated unless
used in its proper scientific sense: subatomic work potential.
In my mother's world, people got sick because of negative energy in their body, and they got better when positive energy
rid their body of toxins. Energy was an all-purpose metaphor
that explained everything from bad relationships to cancer. At
such proclamations, my father would turn his head toward my
mother, his blue eyes sweeping the room like a benevolent light-
house. "What *kind* of energy would that be?" he would ask. "Is
it measurable?"

My father loved my mother with a childlike devotion, and my mother loved him back with a kind of maternal exasperation. She would ask why he couldn't just believe in something he didn't understand, and I would watch my father frown and ponder that question as if it, too, might prove useful in some hyper-rational way. If my mother had really pushed—which she never did—he would probably have answered that believing things you don't understand is either obedience or desperation, and neither leads to the truth. Would we believe in God if we didn't die? Would we believe in energies if all illness was treatable?

My father's mother, Adrienne, was born in Salzburg in 1900 and had twin sisters, much younger, named Ithi and Withi. All three were locally known for their beauty and raised in a well-off family surrounded by some of the most illustrious physicists of the generation. For some reason, a scientific revolution focusing on subatomic particles had begun in the German-speaking world, and many of its luminaries were either from Vienna and Salzburg or traveled there; I have a photograph of my grandmother in a pencil dress and heavy décolletage chatting up Einstein at a cocktail party.

The University of Vienna and the Akademisches Gymnasium had brilliant professors who spawned graduates who went on to become teachers at other universities and spawn another round of graduates. An early Salzburg physicist named Viktor Lang pioneered crystal physics, which begat Franz Exner's work in electrochemistry and radioactivity, which led to Marie and Pierre Curie's isolation of radium. Because their work solved real-world problems, these scientists were considered "applied physicists." They were the garage mechanics of the scientific world; they made things that could be used in everyday life. Carl Welsbach's work on the thorium oxide mantle led to the widespread use of gas streetlamps.

Further out, intellectually, were the theoretical physicists. These men—they were virtually all men—had set out to pry the universe open through the sheer power of their intellects, and their new science proposed a theoretical entity, the atom, that all matter was composed of. Atoms can't be seen directly because they are too small to reflect light, but their existence was the only explanation for things that *could* be seen. And smaller still were the subatomic particles that spun around atomic nuclei like planets orbiting a star. There was nothing smaller in existence and understanding them could be thought of as tantamount to understanding God.

By any measure they were strange men. A story made the rounds of a physicist whose wife told him to change his shirt collar before guests arrived for dinner. The man went up to his bedroom, took off his shirt collar, took off his shirt, continued undressing out of force of habit, climbed into bed, and turned out the light. At least this man was married. Paul Dirac, who discovered antimatter at age twenty-six, found himself on an ocean liner with a young physicist named Werner Heisenberg, who was avidly pursuing the young women on board. In a group not known for good looks or fashion sense, Heisenberg stood out as a brash young exception. When Dirac asked him why he danced in the evenings, Heisenberg replied, "When there are nice girls, it's a pleasure." Dirac thought about this for a moment and then said, "But Heisenberg, how do you know beforehand that they're nice?"

The grandfather of this brilliant madness was Austrian physicist Ludwig Boltzmann, whose proof that gas molecules disperse in proportion to their temperature was foundational to all that followed. Boltzmann showed that molecular movement is simply determined by probability, which results in concentrations of molecules dispersing until they reach equilibrium with their environment. If you pour a potful of boiling water into a cold bath, hot water molecules spread out until they are evenly distributed and have slightly raised the overall bath temperature. Time cannot go backward for the same reason that boiling water can't re-form in one corner of a cold bath and the dead cannot return to life: random probability will never re-concentrate those molecules back into their original form. The branch of physics pioneered by Boltzmann was called statistical mechanics, and it explained one of the fundamental laws of nature: the Second Law of Thermodynamics, also known as entropy.

Boltzmann suffered from depression, and when his work was met with initial skepticism, he went on vacation to a seaside resort, sent his wife and children to play on the beach, and hanged himself in the hotel room. The revolutionary implications of his work only sank in after his death. Boltzmann's chair at the Vienna Institute was filled by one of his students, Fritz Hasenöhrl, whose brilliance was so raw and powerful that he lectured for hours without notes, simply constructing logical truths as he went. When World War One broke out, Hasenöhrl eagerly volunteered to fight and died leading a massed infantry assault on the Tyrolean front.

Left behind was a young student named Erwin Schrödinger, who had listened, awestruck, as Hasenöhrl proved that mass and energy determine each other's values and are therefore the same thing. ("Matter is spirit reduced to the point of visibility—there *is* no matter," as Albert Einstein later put it.) Schrödinger enlisted in the army as well, taking charge of a huge naval gun in the hills above Trieste that was so powerful, his men had to dig it out of the ground after firing it. He was well back from the front line, though, and spent much of his time reading Einstein's latest papers and occasionally entertaining friends from Vienna. He eventually returned to university to pick up where Hasenöhrl had left off.

Because quantum physics could be tested without being understood, it allowed humans to see how the universe worked without knowing why. At that point, physics was so abstract that it bordered on a kind of mysticism. For two hundred years, scientists trusted that the physical world could be understood because it could be measured, but in 1927, Werner Heisenberg demonstrated that subatomic particles changed behavior when observed. That led to staggering questions of whether matter—and reality—was ultimately even knowable. Schrödinger both clarified and deepened the issue by showing that electrons—the foundational unit of existence—were just a series of probabilities that only "collapsed" into one state when measured by humans. As proof, he offered his famous *gedankenexperiment*—thought experiment:

Put a cat in a steel chamber, along with a radioactive isotope that has a 50 percent chance of decaying over the next hour. If it decays, it will release a poison gas that kills the cat. When you open the chamber an hour later, the cat is either alive or dead, but until then, the dead cat and the living cat are statistically smeared together into one "wave function." A wave function is a mathematical description of all possible values for an electron—including existence and nonexistence—and is represented by the Greek letter psi. If a cat could be both there and not there, so could a whole universe, some physicists observed, and there was no way to prove otherwise.

Schrödinger eventually married a Salzburg native named Annemarie Bertel and moved to Switzerland to escape the troubling politics of prewar Austria. He plunged into the study of quantum mechanics while embarking on a series of love affairs that ran parallel to his marriage and professional life without seeming to affect either. Annemarie wasn't troubled by his exertions because she herself had fallen in love with a married German mathematician named Hermann Weyl whose wife, in turn, had fallen in love with a Swiss physicist named Paul Scherrer.

With his marriage and romantic life as background noise, Schrödinger tackled some of the most profound questions of physics. Summoning a mistress from Vienna, he established himself at a chalet in the Swiss resort town of Arosa and proceeded to peel open the world of physics like a sardine can. Over the Christmas holidays of 1925, he discovered the statistical laws governing electrons, which is to say, he wrote a kind of code for all existence. Schrödinger's discoveries stunned the scientific community as if he had communicated with God Himself. After a triumphant speaking tour of German and Swiss research institutes, Schrödinger returned to Zurich, where his wife had helpfully arranged for a pair of beautiful teenage girls to spend the summer. The girls were Ithi and Withi Junger, my father's twin aunts. They were both failing high school math, and Annemarie thought her husband might enjoy tutoring them for the summer. She knew the Junger family from the salons and dinner parties of Salzburg.

The level of math that the girls were failing was so elementary that Schrödinger had to seek the advice of his wife's lover in order to teach it. Over the course of that summer, Schrödinger got Ithi caught up with algebra and also fell in love with her, a passion that was not fully expressed until she was sixteen. Ithi became his principal lover and got pregnant by him, though the situation was quickly terminated by a doctor. Schrödinger was forty-one years old and on his way to being awarded the Nobel Prize in physics.

During all this, Ithi's older sister, Adrienne, married a Spanish-Russian journalist named Jose Chapiro and moved to Dresden, where she gave birth to a boy named Miguel. Almost forty years later, in 1962, that little boy become my father. He lived his entire adult life in Boston and died holding my hand at home at age eighty-nine. Eight years later, in 2020, Miguel Junger appeared in a trauma bay in Hyannis, Massachusetts, statistically smeared like Schrödinger's cat between a state of being and nonbeing, inviting me to join him in the beyond.

The doctors in Hyannis knew I was bleeding massively into my abdomen but didn't know from where. They couldn't fix me until they found that out, but eventually organs fail, the lungs and chest fill with fluid, and the heart stops. You can survive a bad fall or a car accident and suffocate days later from pulmonary edema. My father's sister, Renata, killed herself at age sixteen by throwing herself out an apartment window in New York City in 1947. She fell four stories but landed on the roof of a car, which broke her fall. When she regained consciousness and realized what had happened, she became desperate to live, but it was too late. Her lungs were filled with fluid and there was nothing the doctors could do. Renata died screaming for her mother, who was physically restrained in the next room and calling back to her. Her stepfather sat calmly reading a newspaper until it was over.

The longer they took to find the bleed and stop it, the more blood transfusions I would need and the higher risk I'd run of fatal complications. The alternative was to open me up and simply start looking, but the mortality rate for emergency laparotomy is so high that the doctors later told me they would have brought Barbara to see me. That's not how they would have explained it to her, of course, but every nurse and technician in the OR would have known what the stakes were.

Barbara got to the hospital around nine o'clock. The summer solstice was only a few days away, and there was still a little daylight in the western sky. Moths and June bugs worried the streetlights, and motorboats shifted at their dock lines a block from the hospital. Barbara put on a face mask and hurried into the ER and explained to the reception nurse that Dr. Kohler had told her to come to the hospital. No one knew what to do with her, though, because Covid protocols were still in place and even the dying weren't allowed visitors. (The following morning, by coincidence, those protocols would be suspended.) A nurse finally took her downstairs into what seemed to be a huge basement break room. It was brutally over-air-conditioned and had no cell phone signal. Hospital staff came and went, and whenever Barbara saw someone in scrubs, she would ask about me. In desperation, she even asked a janitor.

Finally, a young woman came through, and Barbara told her that she was waiting for word on her husband. The woman's name was Charlotte, and she was a medical student on a six-week rotation in Hyannis. She remembered that a code crimson had been called earlier that evening—her first blood emergency—and guessed that Barbara was looking for me. "The doctors don't yet know what is wrong with your husband," she said, reaching out to take Barbara's hand. "But they're still searching."

Barbara apologized for taking her time, and Charlotte explained that she wanted to become a doctor so that she could work with people, not parts. "She was a bright light," Barbara said. "Or an angel. I told her I had two little girls at home, and she said that she and her sister were really close, and that it was the very best thing to have two little girls. And that her mother had raised them, and I had this awful feeling that this was a sign. That it would be okay if I had to raise the girls by myself."

The angel left, and more people rotated in and out of the room, and finally a doctor came running through, shouting into his cell phone, "It's the pancreas! It's the pancreas!" Barbara had no idea he was talking about me. The doctor's name was Dan Gorin, and he was the vascular surgeon who had teamed up with an interventional radiologist named Phil Dombrowski. Both had been called in from home. As the hours crept by, Dr. Dombrowski's wife started calling in to make sure he drank enough coffee to stay awake on the drive home.

The rupture was in one of the small arteries—an arcade, as it's called—that supplies blood to the pancreas and duodenum. Had the rupture been in a large abdominal artery, like the aorta, they would have found it a lot faster, but I'd already be dead. Smaller arteries bleed more slowly but are harder to find. My memories from this time are vague and disjointed, as if I had been allowed to see single frames of a very scary movie. I could tell something bad was happening, but not what or why.

Months later, a technician told me I was almost intubated and put on a ventilator when they received me in the interventional radiology suite. "And we kicked a stroke off the table for you," she added. The procedure log shows that I arrived in Cath Lab #3 just after 9:00 p.m., roughly three hours after I started hemorrhaging. Minutes later, I was asked to spell both my names, which were successfully checked against the hospital bracelet on my wrist. I also consented to the procedure that I was about to undergo, though I have no memory of any of this because my blood pressure had just bottomed out at 64 over 59—the border of unconsciousness.

My pulse was also considered "thready," which meant it was weak and hard to find; its opposite is a "bounding" pulse, which seems to leap out of your wrist and can indicate other fatal problems. Your pulse is your life, the ultimate proof you're animate and have something rare to lose. Everything alive has some kind of flux and ebb, and when that stops, life stops. When people say life is precious, they are saying that the rhythmic force that runs through all things—your wrist, your children's wrists, God's entire green earth—is precious. For my whole life, my pulse ran through me with such quiet power that I never had to think about it. And now they were having trouble finding it.

I was lifted and placed on a machine called a fluoroscope that takes real-time moving images by x-ray. At 9:24, the first doctor arrived. Four minutes later, I was "prepped and draped in standard sterile fashion" and transducer levels were zeroed and calibrated. The second doctor arrived, and a male nurse immediately shaved my right groin and swabbed it with disinfectant and lidocaine, which numbs tissue. Two minutes later, Dr. Dombrowski pushed a micro-puncture needle into my femoral artery using an ultrasound probe, as they did with my jugular, and sewed a #5 French sheath into place. I could feel a strange pressure in my groin while they worked but no pain.

The right groin is used as an access point for catheters because most surgeons are right-handed and prefer to stand with their right hand closest to the patient. ("My left hand is basically a flipper," one interventional radiologist admitted to a colleague, who repeated the line to me.) Once the artery port was in place, Dr. Dombrowski slid a microcatheter into my femoral artery and then upstream, against the blood flow, to the abdominal aorta. Catheters are thin wires or tubes that are used to access the interior of the body by navigating the venous system. They have angled tips that allow the surgeon to make a turn into a diverging artery and attachments for performing tasks that would otherwise require abdominal surgery.

Dye had been injected in my veins before the CT scan to illuminate my vascular system, but my abdominal cavity was so full of blood that the surgeons had a hard time pinpointing the leak. The working theory was that I had an aneurysm—painless and undiagnosed—that had grown over years or even decades and eventually ruptured. Had that happened on a camping trip or in a traffic jam or on a transatlantic flight, I would have died. Had I been on blood thinners, I would have died no matter where I was.

The pancreatic artery is an odd place for an aneurysm because blood pressures are much lower than in the aorta, but the doctors noticed an anomaly in my abdomen that might explain it. At the top of the abdominal cavity is a thick bit of gristle called the median arcuate ligament. In most people, the ligament leaves room for the vascular system, but roughly 2 people in 100,000 are diagnosed with a ligament that is too tight. Median arcuate ligament syndrome (MALS) constricts the celiac artery so severely that blood has trouble passing through to digestive organs.

The celiac, which is around an inch wide, is responsible for irrigating the entire abdomen with oxygenated blood. People find out they have MALS because they go to the doctor with digestive problems; the syndrome disproportionately affects women, and digestion can cause so much pain that they wind up with eating disorders. The remedy is to cut the ligament to allow the celiac to expand to normal size or to force it open with a stent, but that can lead to other complications. Scar tissue can recompress the celiac, or the ligament can simply crush the stent.

*My* body, however, had figured out a work-around that allowed me to remain unaware of the problem my entire life. Arteries are strong but elastic and able to dilate under pressure. My celiac was completely occluded—crushed—by the ligament, which had forced blood into smaller arteries that supply the digestive organs. Evolutionary pressure has resulted in a vascular system that is not only resilient but redundant. Throughout the course of my life, those smaller arteries, including the arcade of pancreatic arteries, dilated to handle the increased blood flow from the blocked celiac. It was as if an accident had shut down all three lanes of the Santa Monica Freeway, and drivers were filling residential streets on either side to bypass the blockage.

Surface roads can't expand, but arteries can. They dilate to allow greater blood flow, and my arteries had dilated so successfully that my organs had all the blood they needed. There was no traffic jam in the residential streets, in other words, and I had no reason to suspect anything was wrong. The arteries were extremely twisted and enlarged—during a follow-up exam months later, one technician ran off to get his supervisor when he saw them—but they were doing their job.

In one spot, though, a weakness had resulted in a ballooning outward of the artery wall. The area involved was "the size of a grape," according to one doctor. As the bulge grew, the artery wall became thinner and weaker, which allowed it to expand even more. Pancreatitis can also erode artery walls—pancreatic juices are often likened to battery acid—but I had no symptoms of pancreatitis other than abdominal pain. Most aneurysms are more likely to rupture the larger they get, but this is not true for the pancreatic arcade; small aneurysms are just as deadly as large ones. Of the 131 known cases of true pancreatic aneurysms, around half were diagnosed at the hospital because the artery had already ruptured. Of those, one in four patients died on the table.

The catheter that Dr. Dombrowski had inserted was a #4 French Omniflush that then injected radioactive dye directly into my aorta. The dye showed up on the CT scan and revealed blood backing up in the occluded celiac and pushing into the pancreatic arcade, which was "tortuous" and "enlarged." A microcatheter was placed in three of the enlarged arteries, and Dr. Dombrowski finally determined that the rupture had happened in the "pancreatic branch of the inferior pancreatic-duodenal arcade," a minor and rarely problematic artery. All that remained was to run a catheter down the artery and embolize it with a series of coils that are left in place to create a massive blood clot.

No matter what kind of catheter Dr. Dombrowski used, though, he couldn't navigate the twists and turns of my vasculature. I couldn't just be pumped full of other people's blood indefinitely, and at some point, hard choices had to get made. "Some of this stuff is very scary for the doctors as well," an interventional radiologist told me. "No one wants you to die on their watch . . . no one wants to make the wrong decision and lose an otherwise healthy guy whose wife is waiting in the basement."

I was in and out of consciousness, but I remember telling Dr. Dombrowski and Dr. Gorin that my back was in agony. Blood is exceedingly painful when it comes into contact with internal organs, and my blood had pooled in an area called Morison's pouch, between the kidney and the liver. The procedure log notes that I reported my pain to be "Ten on a scale of one to ten," which surprised me, because acknowledging pain has always seemed vaguely dishonorable, as if it were a kind of personal failure. The pain was on a par with kidney stones or broken bones, and I was reaching the limits of my endurance. My vital signs were too low for general anesthesia, so I was dripped fentanyl and Versed.

The doctors never acknowledged anything I said, but there was a nurse on my left who occasionally held my hand and helped me breathe. At one point I heard her say, "Try to keep your eyes open, Mr. Junger," and when I asked her why, she answered, "So we know you're still with us." *That's an odd thing to say*, I thought. My brain was clumsy and vague, but there was something about the phrase "still with us" that managed to breach the pain and hallucinations and get my attention. In a very distant way, I finally understood that there was something wrong with me that the two gentlemen standing over me might not be able to fix. They might try and try and then simply run out of ideas, and then I would die.

Panicking would have required too much clear thought, but a kind of ancient dread settled over me, as if my body understood what was happening in a way that my mind didn't. And that was when I saw it: a long, significant glance between Dr. Gorin and Dr. Dombrowski. One of them shrugged, and the other just nodded. It wasn't something I was supposed to see, and I couldn't believe that I had. *Tell me you got this*, I thought. *Tell me that whatever is wrong, there's a procedure to fix it, that's what you're going to do, and then I'll go home to my family.*

There *was* a procedure, of course—emergency laparotomy—but Dr. Gorin told me later that he was very much against it. He would have had to cut my abdomen open and excavate my organs until he reached the pancreatic arcade, at which point he would cauterize the ruptured artery and then sew me back up. The look I had seen was very possibly the moment when the two doctors decided there was no way to fix me with a catheter and that they'd have to send me into surgery. I was deeply compromised by six hours of blood loss, though, and there was a decent chance I wouldn't make it.

Then one of the doctors said, "Why don't we try going in through the left wrist?" And the other answered, "I like the way you think." In all likelihood, it was Dr. Dombrowski who thought of the wrist—his business is threading catheters through people's veins—and he is also known for his surgical brilliance. "We call him the magician," was how Dr. Kohler put it. "He went upstream with you because he couldn't get past the celiac artery stenosis. He went backwards. He swam upstream like a salmon."

This would still mean forcing a flexible catheter through my collapsed celiac, but that might allow for a straight shot to the rupture. The arteries leading into my pancreas had been so distorted by excessive blood pressures that they were proving impossible to navigate. At 11:20 p.m., nurses swabbed my left wrist and anaesthetized it with lidocaine, and Dr. Dombrowski slid a micro-puncture needle into the radial artery under ultrasound guidance. A #6 French sheath was inserted into the radial to the subclavian and then down into the abdominal aorta, where a French guide catheter was advanced to the site of the occlusion in the celiac. Dr. Dombrowski forced his way through the blockage with a .014 Quick-Cross catheter and guidewire, and the celiac was then forced open with a balloon catheter. Now, finally, they thought they might be able to reach the rupture.

It was around this time that I started seeing faces in the machinery. I was on a fluoroscope, which allowed Dr. Dombrowski to watch a real-time feed of the catheter moving through my veinous system, and I noticed that the geometry of the overhead arm seemed to contain a human face. Its features were vaguely Aztec in their sternness and glared at me as if I'd committed some mythic betrayal. I tried to look away, but the face was too close and angry to avoid; I was just going to have to pay the price for whatever I'd done.

It was a strangely familiar feeling. Weeks later—long after I'd come back from the hospital—I finally remembered where I'd seen such faces before.

*The fighters converged on us without warning in fiberglass launches powered by huge twin Evinrudes, turning angry circles in the waterway before ramming their boats ashore. They came over the gunnels draped and ready for war with brand-new belt-fed Rachot 68s at their hips and rocket launchers across their backs. They were serious and unhurried, these men, their faces chalked crazily with white paint and their biceps dangling with amulets and fetishes and odd bits of magic to protect them from harm. Some of the face paintings were too deranged to look at for long. One man wore a plaid skirt known as a George and another was naked but for an ammo belt and dirty white briefs. The rest were in cast-off camouflage and T-shirts and fabric that could hardly be named as clothing. They were a collection of walking nightmares, everything terrifying to the human psyche, and when confronted with them, Nigerian soldiers have been known to drop their weapons and run.*

*They were Ijaw warriors from the Movement for the Emancipation of the Niger Delta, and their leader was a slender boy in a white robe and red turban who was helped out of the boat almost as if he were a child. He had been chosen in a dream by Egbesu, their god of war, to lead his fellow warriors in combat. Egbesu told some men to lead for a day and others to lead for months, and if the chosen man told the truth, the others obeyed him without question. If he lied, Egbesu killed him. Egbesu's sole concern was truth and justice, and the Ijaw understood that those goals sometimes require violence.*

*I was with an American photographer named Mike and an Ogoni woman who knew the area, and when the young leader approached, we shot to our feet like penitent schoolboys. He handed his rifle to another man without bothering to look at him and asked which one of us was Sebastian. "I am," I said. He handed me a cell phone and said that Jomo was on the line. Jomo was the leader of MEND and rumored to be in South Africa, three thousand miles away. "I told you that you couldn't go out into the creeks," Jomo said. I started to explain, but Jomo cut me off and told me to spell my last name. I was standing on a log, trying to preserve the last bar of cell phone service connecting me to Jomo, and I spelled out my name as calmly as possible. "I'm going to call Ijaw people in New York to inquire about you," he said. "Don't worry, everything's going to be all right."*

*I handed the phone back to the leader and then rejoined Mike in front of a thatch hut. The village was so poor they didn't even have galvanized for roofing. After a few minutes, one of the young men strode up and pointed a finger at my face. He was short but extremely strong and his entire body was painted white. "You," he said. "I am going to kill you."*

*Whatever happens, stay standing, I thought; do not let your knees buckle. The man stared at me and then walked off. We waited and smoked cigarettes and watched the men for the slightest sign they might warm up to us or at least decide we weren't a threat. MEND was disrupting the global oil supply by storming offshore platforms and blowing up pipelines, and they assumed it was only a matter of time before the Americans came after them. And then Mike and I showed up. After a while Jomo called back and told his men to let us go. My name had checked out with his Ijaw friends in New York, whatever that meant.*

*One of the men had taken my windbreaker, and I walked up to him and told him to give it back. Not that I cared about the windbreaker, but it seemed important that they not realize how terrified we were. Weeks later, in New York, I opened my eyes to see my entire bedroom ceiling covered in Ijaw war paint. I lay there staring and paralyzed until the vision receded. You cannot visit a place of such violence and death and not expect it to follow you home, I thought; you cannot seek out another man's suffering and not become part of it. One day it will paint your ceiling and fill your mind and hijack your dreams. One day it will appear on hospital equipment above your head when there is nothing left to do but hope Egbesu hasn't decided you were lying the entire time.*

The venous catheter was invented by a young German doctor named Werner Forssmann at a small Red Cross hospital outside Berlin in 1929. He had become obsessed with the idea of accessing the heart without surgery, via an artery, but medical wisdom at the time considered the heart too delicate to survive such an intrusion. It was thought that anything touching the interior of the heart would trigger cardiac arrest. Unable to convince the senior doctor at his hospital to use the technique on a patient, Forssmann suggested trying it on someone who was dying. When that idea was shot down, Forssmann decided to perform the procedure on himself.

He needed an assistant, so he lured a hospital nurse into his scheme. The woman, Gerda Ditzen, assumed that Dr. Forssmann would perform the secret procedure on her and was thrilled to be the first person to have a rubber catheter inserted into her heart chambers. One day when there were no surgeries scheduled for the hospital, he told Ditzen to bring a sterilized scalpel, a large-gauge needle, and a ureteral catheter to the operating bay. Ureteral catheters, used to drain urine from the kidneys, were both thin enough to fit inside a vein and long enough to reach the heart.

Ditzen sterilized the equipment and followed Forssmann into the surgery bay, where he strapped her down on the operating table and then stepped behind her, out of sight. According to

Forssmann's own account, he swabbed the interior of his elbow with iodine and injected Novocain into the area, and then did the same to Ditzen, so she wouldn't suspect anything. By then the anesthetic had taken effect, and he used a scalpel to make an incision down to the antecubital vein in his elbow and then slid the needle into it. Working quickly, he inserted the catheter into the needle and then started pushing it up his vein, toward his heart.

When he estimated that the tube had reached his shoulder, Forssmann walked around the operating table so that Ditzen could see him. (Decades later, he told Dr. Lawrence Altman that she was furious about it.) "It's done," he said, and told her to accompany him to the radiology lab. Using a fluoroscope and a mirror to guide himself, he pushed the catheter all the way into the chambers of his own heart and then ordered the radiographer to take a photograph. Finally, he had proof that catheters could penetrate deep into the human body.

The essential challenge of navigating the venous system with long rubber tubes is turning into smaller veins and arteries that are often at right angles. Catheters must be flexible enough to go around corners but stiff enough to push through resistance. To accomplish this bit of magic, guide catheters are equipped with a slightly curved "cobra" head that can be rotated into a branching artery—from the celiac into the pancreaticoduodenal, for example—and then pushed in a new direction. For extreme maneuvers, a "shepherd's crook" can be hooked into an acute angle and pushed into a collateral vessel that is effectively heading in the opposite direction. Once the guide catheter is established, a larger "superfeed" catheter can be run through and used as a work tunnel for smaller catheters that can go in and out doing the actual work: inflating balloons, embolizing ruptures, inserting stents, and injecting radioactive dyes.

My pancreatic artery was so tortuous that even after Dr. Dombrowski forced open the celiac with a balloon catheter, he still couldn't reach the rupture. Fortunately, human vasculature is so redundant that you can get to any organ from multiple directions. One of the primary tasks of our vascular system is to not bleed to death—hence clotting factors, spontaneous arterial repair, and arteries buried deep inside our bodies—but another is to make sure our organs get plenty of blood. That means that Dr. Dombrowski would be able to try one last approach. According to the medical summary, he pushed his catheter "via the inferior pancreaticoduodenal branch of the superior mesenteric artery" into "the medial collateral vessel arising from the proximal splenetic artery."

The splenetic artery had thwarted his previous attempts, but from this new angle, Dr. Dombrowski finally reached the site of active bleeding. Because the artery was open to blood flow from both directions, he would have to block both ends—the "front door" and the "back door." He used micro-coils that resemble tiny pipe cleaners and provide an armature for blood clots. The clots start to form in minutes and eventually turn into a dense mass of dead blood and scar tissue. Coils have been known to shift, leak, rebleed, and even get flushed farther down the artery, so doctors scan the area afterward to make sure everything has stayed in place. But around one o'clock on the morning of

June 17, 2020, Dr. Dombrowski pulled his gear out of my radial artery, closed my groin entry with a Celt closure, and noted that the bleeding in my abdomen had stopped. The procedure log notes that at 1:20 a.m., "Physicians broke scrub, invasive procedure complete."

Biologically, I should have died six months into the fifty-ninth year of my life, but I didn't. Dr. Dombrowski, Dr. Gorin, the hospital staff, and a gallery of odd and brilliant obsessives who pioneered things like blood transfusion and venous catheterization kept that from happening. I was in the first generation in history that could reliably be saved from abdominal hemorrhage. After seeing the terrible visages emerge from the machinery, my next memory was of Barbara in a hallway. She had been summoned from the basement waiting room by a clutch of weary doctors and medical staff. They told her that I was stable but would have to be taken straight to the ICU.

My back was still in agony, and all I could think was that my pleas had gone ignored by the medical staff. Barbara was my last hope. "Please rub my back," I whispered, thinking the nurses wouldn't hear me, but one of them shook her head. "Just a little," I begged.

They rolled me into a big hospital elevator and brought me up to the ICU. A ring of darkened rooms surrounded a central nursing station, and in that darkness slept the sickest people in the hospital. I joined them. Barbara sat next to me and held my hand until I fell asleep, and then a nurse told her to go home and get some rest. Barbara made her way to the nearly empty parking lot and drove home through a ground fog so thick that it removed almost all details of the world except the double yellow line that flicked under her wheels.

I had no dreams in the ICU but seemed to wallow in a broad featureless dark that was finally punctured by the voices of two women above me. They came from far away and had Boston accents and were discussing a very ill man, which turned out to be me. I opened my eyes. "Good morning, Mr. Junger," one of them said. She peered down at me in my bed, which had guardrails and a side table. A welter of cables led from my chest to a machine above my head. A bright prospect of Hyannis Harbor offered itself through the windows, and a big, pale summer day. I flashed a dim memory of the previous night as a cluster of strange and eager gargoyles waiting for me to give in. "You almost died last night," the nurse said. "In fact, no one can believe you're alive."

After a few minutes the nurses continued their rounds, and I found myself alone again. A hot June day was building outside the windows, and I could hear heavy equipment moving around at a construction site somewhere below. *If I'd died, all this would be still happening, except that I'd be in a refrigeration unit downstairs,* I thought. I tried to imagine how Xana would understand the news. Daddy died? Yes, sweetheart. When is he coming back? Never. Why not? Because he's dead. Why can't he come back if he's dead?

Because everything was new to her, Xana saw things with extraordinary clarity; we actually have no idea what the dead can and can't do. Once, after visiting a New York City firehouse, she asked me why the firemen were so small. That stumped me— they were all pretty big, and one was truly a giant.

"They're not small, they're big," I answered. Xana thought about that for a moment.

"Not compared to the buildings they go into," she said.

Xana had somehow summarized our relationship with a vast universe that doesn't seem to care or even notice if we die. How could I have almost died on an ordinary June day in perfectly good health? I remembered the ambulance ride, but that didn't explain much, because I hadn't felt very sick. Then I remembered the trauma bay, but that didn't help, either; hadn't I been joking around with the doctors? Finally, I remembered Dr. Wilson's face upside down above me, asking permission to pierce my neck. "In case there's an emergency?" I'd asked. "This *is* the emergency," he replied. Then he asked if I was claustrophobic, and when I said yes, he said, "Well, that's too bad," and draped a plastic sheet over my face. Finally, someone with a sense of humor! And then, reluctantly, I remembered the great darkness that had started tugging at me from below. "Hurry up, Doc, you're losing me," I remembered telling Wilson. "I'm going right now."

And eventually I remembered my father. I'd been conscious enough to be talking to the doctor, which meant I was conscious enough to be puzzled by the appearance of a dead person on the ceiling—especially my dad, who was somehow urging me to stop struggling and go with him. *The darkness is going to win*, he seemed to be saying. *You don't need to fight it. You can come with me.*

I lay there trying to pin down the memory of my father. Occasionally the phone rang at the nursing station, or a patient went by with a nurse, dragging an IV pole behind him, but otherwise, the ICU was quiet. I lay there thinking about death for the first time in my life. Not death on my terms—the jacked-up energy of a close call, the sick relief of a lucky break—but on *its* terms. The great gaping pit that has everything and nothing inside it, including your dead father. It's not in a hurry because it doesn't have to be; it's just there. You're the one in the hurry, rushing this way and that, and then suddenly the pit is swallowing you and the room and the world and all the light in it. I thought about *that* version of death for the first time. The version that isn't a thing; the version that is absolutely nothing.

My back was still in agony, and I thought it might feel better if I rolled onto my side. It took all my will to accomplish this, and I had to bring the tangle of cables with me. One IV went to my right arm and half a dozen monitors were pasted to my chest, which had been shaved for that purpose. The information showed up as a series of jagged ups and downs on a monitor above my head. Later that morning my abdomen convulsed without warning and a spectacular jet of dark blood arced out of my mouth and soaked the bed. It must have been audible from the corridor, because a nurse said, "Oh dear," and then there was a rush of activity, and two women were rolling me from one side to the other to change the sheets.

The nurse who had told me I'd almost died came back for a visit about an hour later. She was middle-aged and gave the impression of being compassionate but also very businesslike, as if dying was not a particularly big deal and you might not want to be overly dramatic about it. She asked how I was doing. "I'm okay," I lied. "But I can't believe I almost died last night. It's terrifying."

She considered me for a moment. "Instead of thinking of it as something scary," she said, "try thinking of it as something sacred."

*Eventually we will all behold the void. I was twenty and it was compelling because it was terrifying, and I was determined that it shouldn't be. The road ended for good at an outpost town called Guelmim, on the northern edge of the Sahara, and beyond that were a thousand miles of desert. It was raining slightly and very cold. There were no tourists or cops or hotels in Guelmim, just young men smoking hashish and glum-looking soldiers. The soldiers were battling desert nomads known as the Polisario for control of a strange empty territory called Western Sahara, and the king of Morocco had recently decided to solve the problem by bulldozing an 800-mile sand berm into the desert. I was traveling with a woman named Sarah, whom I'd known my whole life. We weren't cousins or siblings but might as well have been. It was almost dark, and we stepped into the first boardinghouse we saw, but a blond kid caught my eye through the smoke and slatted light and shook his head.*

*We stepped back into the rain and found another boardinghouse that felt safer. We slept in our clothes and started walking south early in the morning. It very much felt as if we were leaving port and sailing out to sea. We walked past unfinished concrete buildings at the edge of town and piles of garbage smoldering in the acrid morning and boys playing soccer on dirt pitches and silent women staring from behind veils. Finally, we were in the desert and moving south across an ochre hardpan toward a series of hills. The vegetation was low and dead-looking, and we crossed a broad wash that was invisible until we were right on top of it, and then walked through the morning to gain a rock outcrop we'd spotted an hour earlier. From there we stood at the edge of a vast flat basin that ran to the edges of the horizon, and far off in that valley was a scattering of camels and a lone brown tent. It was a nomad's tent with two supports and its front flap propped up. A light tail of smoke drifted out of the camp, and we came down off the outcrop through its skirts of fine red sand and set out to see what it was.*

*Guelmim was the largest camel market in southern Morocco, and the men who brought their animals north to sell were Sahrawis who lived beyond the reach of government authority. They were descendants of Arab marauders named the Benu Hilal and Beni Salama who had emigrated from Egypt in the eleventh century. They preyed on the gold and slave caravans moving along the great sand routes and fought off the local Berber tribes and eventually established a vast and fluid domain that recognized no outside power or colonial law. The Sahrawi were known to dress in fine blue fabric that left a sheen on their skin, and the men went armed with rifles and pistols and knives, and the women went unveiled, unlike the wives of farmers and merchantmen to the north. They made silver jewelry to trade in the desert towns and slaved and raided and drove herds for their livelihoods and lived in camel-hair tents that could be raised or dismantled in an hour. Some were as pale as Europeans and considered the upper class of Sahrawi society, and others were smaller and darker and worked as servants because of their origins farther south in Mali and Niger.*

Two men stood to greet us as we approached. Their tent was brown and tan and stretched over two crossed poles and weighed down at the edges by rocks. A stick propped the front open and a crude wood-and-leather camel saddle sat at the entrance. The men seemed neither worried nor threatening and held their hands empty, as did we. They waved us over to the fire and set a teapot to boil as per custom, and we sat cross-legged and nodded and smiled. Sarah knew a little Arabic and they knew a little French, but our hands waved about and did most of the talking. One man was tall and light-skinned and very handsome, almost like a movie star, and the other was older and darker. The handsome man seemed to be the dominant of the two and he filled four tin cups with a high elaborate pour and passed each one out delicately because the cups were hot and had no handles. Then he handed out cigarettes and lit them for us, and we drank tea and smoked tobacco and tried to explain ourselves.

It was midafternoon, and Sarah and I were running out of time to make it back to town. The handsome man pointed to the east and made a motion of the sun rising—tomorrow, we figured— and then pointed at Sarah and me and made a beckoning sign. He was inviting us to return. We walked back to town in the hurrying dusk and packed tangerines and blocks of chocolate and rounds of flatbread and set out the next afternoon just before sunset. Night came fast and we found ourselves steering into a dark emptiness that had neither stars nor town lights to guide by. Only the crunch of our boots in the gravel let us know that we existed. Eventually we saw a strange orange star on the horizon that seemed to draw closer *as we walked, and soon we came out of the darkness into the familiar circle of their firelight.*

*The headman sat us down and immediately asked for English lessons while the other tended the fire. The cook had worked up a fine vegetable stew and when the prayers were over, he set it before us in a big clay tajine that we ate from communally in the fashion of the desert. There was nothing in the tent that had not come from the desert except a plastic water jug and a flintlock musket. The musket was to protect the camels.*

*The front of the tent was dropped for the night, and Sarah and I were shown to a pile of goatskin bedding. We were assumed to be married and didn't say otherwise. Before we went to sleep, the headman explained that in five days they would travel south to rejoin their people in the desert and would be back to Guelmim in half a year with another herd of camels to sell. If we wanted to join him, he would consider us his personal guests. I went to sleep to the sound of him practicing his new language out loud by candlelight.*

*Morning. A gray void. Everyone asleep around me. I unroll myself from the goatskins and step outside. A north wind has swept away the clouds and the great cast of stars overhead are fading in their fastenings. I start running across the desert in my jeans and sweater, heading east toward the coming day. Before we went to sleep, Sarah said she could not stay but would explain everything to my parents if I decided to, and now I'm running across the desert to find out what it will be. Am I the kind of person who will disappear into the desert with Sahrawi camel traders for six months or am I not? It seemed like a fundamental difference between people. I run for a mile or two and stop on a low rise that grants a view of where I've come. It takes a moment to even pick out the tent. Oh God, thy sea is so great and my boat is so small, as the prayer goes.*

*I have the feeling that whatever I choose, I will make that same choice for the rest of my life. If I gamble everything to find out what I don't know, then I will always do that. If I turn back, I will always turn back. Is the unknown a place of mystery or terror? Am I sufficient unto myself or eternally indentured to my origins?*

*It turns out that the desert has no insights into me that I don't already know. I trot off the hill and back across the flatland as a cold winter sun rises behind me. The headman is reclined in his djellaba, smoking a cigarette and shouting out his morning prayers. He is using his new vocabulary, though, so "God-u-akbar! God-u-akbar!" rings out across the desert. Sarah and I pack our bags and hug each of the men and give them a Swiss Army knife, which they are still studying as we start north. We leave one version of ourselves behind and pick up where we'd left off with the old versions, our more courageous doubles now forever condemned to our imaginations and what might have been.*

Barbara arrived late in the morning and I watched her walk up to the bed and kneel to be at my level. Her face was a map of fear and relief and exhaustion. "You seemed very weak, like a changed person," she told me later. "There was something haunted about you—the specter of death. You seemed weakened in a way that I didn't know if you'd ever recover."

Barbara stayed all day, watching me drift in and out of

consciousness. I was in a lot of pain and could not carry a coherent conversation. We called my sister, in England, but I was exhausted and out of breath after a few words. Occasionally, Barbara would walk around the ICU floor and ask questions of the nursing staff, and she noticed that she was getting looked at in a particular way. *This is what happens to widows—this is the look they get,* she thought. As if she were now in a different category because she had been brushed by death.

During that first hour, in and out of sensibility, I told Barbara about the black pit and my father. During the ensuing months I came to doubt my memory—and even wondered if I'd made the whole thing up—but Barbara confirmed that it was one of the first things I talked about. "You were trying to put together everything that happened," she said. "You remembered it sequentially. You saw the pit and you got out the word to the living people around you, that something was pulling you away. As if you were hanging off a window ledge looking down. And you told me, *My dad was there.* You were so surprised and puzzled. It didn't seem like a good thing or a bad thing; it just seemed like a fact."

Barbara had spent six hours in the hospital basement waiting for the high priests of medicine to tell her whether she still had a husband, but she did not truly understand how close I'd come until we spoke. "The pit—*you're losing me*—seeing your dead father—it all just finally clunked into my brain that you were going to die," she said. "It doesn't surprise me that you saw the dead. Not because I have strong beliefs about it, but because I have zero disbelief."

That first day, Barbara knew I could easily still die; her older sister had received a stent for a dissecting aortic aneurysm and died in her sleep a few days later. I could die of a stroke or a pulmonary embolism or pulmonary edema or any number of transfusion reactions. When Dr. Gorin stopped by to see how I was doing, Barbara asked if there were any ongoing threats to my life.

"No," he said. "We transfused him, found the problem, and fixed it."

He may well have said that for my benefit. With a lot of help from Barbara and the nurse, I finally managed to sit on the edge of the bed. The effort required was so extraordinary that I felt as if I'd broken some kind of world record. I said good-bye to Barbara easily, the way people do when they're not thinking about dying, and then I lay there and resumed thinking about dying. Suppose I'd gone running in the woods instead of staying home? Suppose I had sent the paramedics away instead of going to the hospital? And as the evening sky paled and then turned orange and blue and the harbor lights came on outside my window, I found I couldn't avoid memories of death itself. I'd beheld it. Felt it. Started to become it. My worst fear—other than dying—was that because I'd come so close to death, it would now accompany me everywhere like some ghastly pet. Or, more accurately, I was now the pet, and my new master was standing mutely with the lead watching me run out the clock.

It's an open question whether a full and unaverted look at death crushes the human psyche or liberates it. One could say that it's the small ambitions of life that shred our souls, and that if we're lucky enough to glimpse the gargoyles of our final descent and make it back alive, we are truly saved. Every object is a miracle compared to nothingness and every moment an infinity when correctly understood to be all we'll ever get. Religion does its best to impart this through a lifetime of devotion, but one good look at death might be all you need.

When the American writer Herman Melville shipped out on a whale-hunting ship named the *Acushnet* in 1841, there was a black man aboard named John Backus who was famous for having once leapt out of a chase boat in panic. His fellow crew members had to suspend the hunt to save him. *Acushnet* means "peaceful resting place by the water" in Wampanoag, but in reality, each whale ship was its own brutal world. The industry killed men by the score, captains were often deranged sadists, and crew members would jump overboard at the first sight of land. Melville himself abandoned ship in the Marquesas Islands and was captured by cannibals, who held him for four months before giving him up to an Australian whaler.

John Backus is thought to be the basis for a character named Pippin in Melville's epic novel *Moby-Dick*. Pip, as he is called, is a young black man who serves as cabin boy on the fictional whaleship the *Pequod*. One day, Pip is pressed into service on a chase boat, but as soon as a whale has been harpooned, Pip panics and jumps overboard. The harpooner, a man named Stubb, is forced to cut the line—and lose the whale—so that Pip won't die. He warns Pip, however, that next time he will choose the whale.

"But we are all in the hands of the Gods," as Melville observed. "Pip jumped again." True to his word, Stubb does not cut the line, and the chase boat is quickly hauled out of sight by the whale. Pip finds himself in a warm, calm sea, swimming effortlessly but completely alone. There are three miles of water beneath him and the vaulting sky above and not a single living thing in sight. An hour passes, and by some freakish chance, the *Pequod* comes upon him, and the crew haul him aboard. Though Pip is alive, he has seen God and been rendered imbecile. "The sea had jeeringly kept his finite body up, but drowned the infinite of his soul," Melville writes. "Not drowned entirely, though. Rather carried down alive to wondrous depths . . . He saw God's foot upon the treadle of the loom, and spoke it; and therefore his shipmates called him mad. So man's insanity is heaven's sense."

After that, Pip walked the decks of the *Pequod* offering a reward for himself, as if he were an escaped slave who needed to be caught and returned home.

# IF

In July 2012, a combat medic named Tyler Carroll deployed to Logar Province in eastern Afghanistan. Carroll was with First Battalion, Dog Company of the 173rd Airborne Brigade, and his unit's mission was to circulate through the area packing up American bases. Every day one platoon would handle perimeter security, one platoon would patrol the area, and one platoon would dismantle the base and act as a quick reaction force. As a medic, Carroll was trained to fight alongside everyone else until someone was shot or blown up, at which point he would put his rifle down and open up his first aid bag.

Occasionally a firefight is so intense that medics find themselves fighting and attending to the wounded at the same time. Occasionally medics find themselves attending to the wounded even though they are wounded themselves. Badly wounded medics have died trying to instruct other soldiers how to save someone else's life or their own. The prospect of failing to save a fellow soldier is so devastating many medics fear that more than dying, and the inevitable casualties of combat can cause medics a lifetime of trauma and guilt.

Dog Company was a heavy-weapons unit that was supposed to move around in armored combat vehicles, but the terrain was so rugged that they mostly patrolled on foot. That made them vulnerable to Taliban fighters in the high ground, and the men of Dog Company found themselves taking plunging fire from the ridgelines almost every day. One afternoon, Carroll's platoon was doing live-fire drills at a small base in Kherwar District when a rocket-propelled grenade streaked overhead and exploded next to a soldier named Jason Moss. Carroll sprinted over, grabbed Moss by the drag-strap on his body armor, and pulled him into a nearby shipping container. The thin steel of the container could never stop a bullet but would offer a little concealment from the Taliban fighters above. Three other soldiers followed Carroll, and as soon as they made it inside, another explosion engulfed them. This time it was from a 40mm mortar that tore a hole in the shipping container and sprayed everyone inside with jagged spears of metal.

Carroll peered through the dust and saw that every other man was down. *Shit, they're all dead*, he thought. "I'm not scared at all," Carroll says. "It's the weirdest thing. I'm not scared at all, I'm totally calm. It was this surreal confidence and clarity."

Carroll asked who could stand up, and several men struggled to their feet. The wounded were moaning and men outside were screaming directions and the entire base was erupting in automatic weapons fire. Carroll asked if anyone could walk, and a man named Armando Alvarado said that he could. Carroll told Alvarado to sprint to the base command center to get a litter team. Alvarado took off running despite having a shrapnel wound in his chest that punctured his lung; by the time he got to the command center fifty yards away, he was coughing up blood and actively dying. Back at the shipping container, Jason Moss was holding his leg and bleeding out.

As Carroll began to treat Moss, he realized that another soldier named Theodore Glende was also wounded. Glende was unconscious on the ground, and Moss started yelling at Carroll to help Glende first. "I go over to my buddy Glende and I'm shaking him and he's not making a sound," says Carroll. "He's lifeless—that stare, I can recognize it immediately. I had never seen a dead person until that moment, but I could just tell. He was staring off into a completely different reality."

Carroll stripped off Glende's body armor and shirt and several liters of blood came tumbling out of him. (Medics would later discover that a tiny sliver of shrapnel had entered between his shoulder blades and severed his aorta, killing him almost immediately.) Drenched in Glende's blood, Carroll noticed what he thought was an abdominal organ lying next to him on the ground. He picked it up, wondering who it came from, and then put it back down and continued trying to save Glende's life. No carotid pulse, no radial pulse, no response to anything. Carroll tried to roll Glende over to examine his back but found he couldn't do it because his left arm didn't work. He couldn't move it at all. Another soldier looked at Carroll and said, "Doc, you don't look so good."

"That's when the huge wave hit me," Carroll says. "I'm hurt. Glende's dead. My other buddy is dying. This is all my responsibility, and I need to perform."

As it turned out, Carroll was bleeding out as well. Shrapnel had shredded his shoulder, and the human tissue next to him in the shipping container was actually part of his own rear deltoid. He was still conscious, though, and decided to start CPR and an IV on Glende and an IV on Moss. Just as he started pulling gear out of his first aid bag, he slumped over, unconscious. A few moments later he woke up, continued working, passed out, and then woke up again. Carroll's memories of working on his dead friend were seamless and uninterrupted, and he had no idea that he was cycling through periods of unconsciousness.

"There were a lot of times that I was unconscious on my knees," Carroll says. "I would wake back up and go back to treating my friend and not even realize that I am dying."

During this neurological twilight, Carroll had an extraordinary vision. His entire life presented itself to him simultaneously and in great detail, as if twenty-one years of experience could co-exist outside linear time. "My whole life flashed before my eyes, from birth to the present moment," Carroll says. "I thought of my wife. I thought of my mom. I thought of how much love I had for them. And then there'd be a sudden rush—no, no, wake up! And I'd start trying to treat Glende again. *I'm the medic, I need to survive in order for these guys to survive.* And then my inner reality again: *It's okay. Let go. You were loved. You loved them. Nothing else matters.* There was just this total acceptance of what was happening."

Carroll had gone into hemorrhagic shock, and when the litter team arrived, they found him so pale and bloodless that his
skin was translucent. The senior medic asked Carroll if he was
okay, and he woke up and said, "Glende has a small wound on
his back, just an inch from his spine, Moss has a femoral bleed,"
and then went back to sleep. Every time they woke him up, Carroll gave the same medical report and then went to sleep again.
The team lifted Carroll onto the litter and carried him back to
the schoolhouse and started to treat him in the hallway. They
packed his wounds and ran an IV and called in a medevac and
watched in alarm as Carroll's body started spasming. He was
entering hypothermia, his body's last-ditch effort to stay alive.
A Blackhawk helicopter landed at the base, and the wounded
men were loaded on. Glende was dead, but Moss, Carroll, and
Alvarado had a chance. The helicopter took off and received
ground fire as soon as it was airborne. Carroll saw a mountain
ridge swing past, out the bay door, and thought, *If we make it
over that, we'll survive.*

C arroll's vision has been named a "life review" by researchers
who study the subjective experience of dying. Advances in
modern medicine have regularly allowed people to "come back
from the dead," as it were, and many who do report extraordinary visions and experiences from their trip to the other side. A
Dutch study of 344 people who survived cardiac arrest found that
between 12 and 18 percent had deep and affecting experiences
on the threshold of life: meeting dead loved ones, being ushered
through a tunnel of light, existing outside of their bodies, and

being filled with love and bliss. The life review is one of the most powerful and comforting of these visions. It is characterized by the conviction that you have sweeping knowledge of all things and can simultaneously reexperience your entire life. "When my expansion was over, I was everywhere, I was everything at the same time," one woman recalled. "I was the sky, I was the ground, I was the trees, and I felt the wind blowing in my leaves, I was the sea and I was also my parents, my friends, people I had not met before but who, at that point, I knew because they were part of me."

A former wildland firefighter named Ken Senn told me that he suffered an abdominal hemorrhage while hunting with his son in the Bitterroot Mountains of Montana. His son, Caleb, had already dislocated his shoulder trying to help his father over rough ground, so the two men were forced to spend the night by a fire in subfreezing temperatures hoping rescuers would find them before they died. Ken was semi-functional from blood loss and Caleb was deep in shock from an unreduced shoulder. At dawn, Caleb set out to try to make it to a road. "After Caleb left, I was at peace because I knew he was going to be okay," Senn said. "But I knew I was dying. And that was when the mountains started to move, started to ripple. And I realized that the entire world was alive, everything was alive. And I saw all these animals below me and they were all dying, and I knew I was going to die too, one day, but we were all linked. And I felt at peace because I knew my body belonged to the earth. The Angel of Death was whispering in my ear."

The similarity with many religious experiences is striking. Renowned yogi Paramahansa Yogananda describes the moment of his enlightenment as a young student in India: "Soul and mind instantly lost their physical bondage and streamed out like a fluid . . . the flesh was as though dead; yet in my intense awareness I knew that never before had I been fully alive. My sense of identity was no longer narrowly confined to a body but embraced the circumambient atoms. People on distant streets seemed to be moving gently over my own remote periphery. The roots of plants and trees appeared through a dim transparency of the soil; I could discern the inward flow of their sap . . . A swelling glory within me began to envelop towns, continents, the earth, solar and stellar systems, tenuous nebulae, and floating universes."

Yogananda went on to be received by President Calvin Coolidge as one of the most important religious figures of the new century. Some researchers point to similarities between so-called near-death experiences and religion as evidence of an afterlife, but it's equally possible that religions have those traits precisely because that's how people experience dying. For hundreds of thousands of years, presumably, people have returned from the twilight world of hemorrhagic shock and low blood oxygen to report meeting the dead, hovering over their own bodies, and experiencing universal consciousness. Those experiences could be entirely the result of neurochemical changes in the dying brain but still mistaken for actual trips into the afterlife. A worldwide belief in spirits could then develop that involved a special caste of shamans, priests, and sorcerers who ferried messages back and forth between the tiny, beautiful world of the living and the vast tracts of the dead.

Little is known about what happens in the brain of a dying person, but researchers in Estonia got the chance in 2022. An eighty-seven-year-old man fell, struck his head, and suffered a subdural hematoma. Surgeons at the University of Tartu relieved pressure on the brain by cutting a hole in his skull, but the patient developed epilepsy and lapsed into a coma. Doctors attached electrodes to his skull to monitor electrical activity in his brain but were unable to save him. He suffered cardiac arrest and was not revived, in accordance with his family's wishes. The electrodes, however, gave researchers a first-ever look at the electrical activity of a dying human brain.

During the thirty seconds before and after death, the patient's brain experienced a surge of gamma waves associated with memory retrieval, intense concentration, dissociative states, and dreaming. Laboratory rats experience the same surge of gamma waves when they die. The flood of memories experienced by Tyler Carroll as he drifted in and out of consciousness at a forward operating base in Afghanistan may be a trait common to all mammals, and the evolutionary advantage may simply lie in providing one last, compelling motivation to stay alive.

Military researchers have also produced similar memories and visions by accelerating fighter pilots to unconsciousness in human centrifuges. Gravity-induced loss of consciousness—G-LOC—starts to occur at accelerations of five times the force of gravity, and modern fighter planes can achieve almost twice that in less than a second. Under those conditions, a 200-pound man effectively weighs almost one ton. Losing consciousness while flying a fighter plane at twice the speed of sound is obviously catastrophic, and Air Force researchers have accelerated test pilots to unconsciousness more than a thousand times to determine the limits of human performance. "You cannot die without losing consciousness," Dr. James

Whinnery observed in a paper titled "Psychophysiologic Correlates of Unconsciousness and Near-Death Experiences." Winnery goes on to write: "Everyone should, therefore, have some interest in loss of consciousness since he or she will experience it at least once."

The reason pilots lose consciousness under high G-forces is that blood is forced into the abdomen and other flexible areas of the body, and the heart is not powerful enough to pump it back out. First, pilots experience "grayout" of their vision, then tunnel vision, then complete blindness, and finally memory loss. At that point they are completely unconscious and experiencing brief, surreal reveries similar to what Tyler Carroll experienced. And like Carroll, they have no understanding that they are passing in and out of consciousness. One man thought he was floating in a warm ocean under a beautiful yellow sun; another left the testing center still feeling like he was "above and behind himself, watching his own body walking."

Cardiac arrest does the same thing as G-LOC, but if circulation does not resume within minutes, brain cells start to die. First responders use "ambubags"—a mechanical substitute for mouth-to-mouth resuscitation—to force oxygen into the lungs, and chest compressions to force blood through the body. That keeps the brain irrigated with enough oxygenated blood to stave off cell death. At the hospital, doctors shock cardiac victims with a defibrillator, put them on a ventilator to help them breathe, inject them with adrenaline, and finally cut their chests open to try to massage their heart back to life. The survival rate for cardiac arrest is about 10 percent.

Doctors will tell you that a person lives or dies because of biology—organ failure, cell necrosis, blood loss—but many survivors say they remember it as a "decision." They claim to remember looking *down* at the doctors who are trying to save them, often in puzzlement, and don't even recognize the dying body as their own. What doctors, nurses, and family members take to be a tragic end point, the dying often experience as an infinite expansion. The dying often say that they reentered their bodies only because the living still needed them.

I have a friend who, in her midseventies, suffered cardiac arrest in a car accident. It was a head-on collision with both cars going forty miles an hour, and my friend says she has no memory of impact; one moment she was driving, the next moment, she was running through a field of beautiful flowers. "I was rushing toward two long-dead friends I hadn't thought about in years," she told me. "My arms were open, and I was full of joy, but just before I reached them, I felt myself yanked back into my body."

The medics had just defibrillated her. By some miracle, she had crashed directly in front of the fire station of her little town.

When I had my visions, my heart was beating, and I was still talking to the doctors. Instead of rising above my body or joyfully reuniting with loved ones, a black pit opened up that my dead father tried to escort me through. Even more upsetting, though, was the dream I'd had thirty-six hours prior to almost dying. My wife and children were below me but forever beyond my reach, and I was headed into an infinite void that apparently now owned me and would never let me return.

My father died of congestive heart failure at eighty-nine, and a few days before he passed, I was awoken in the middle of the night by a similarly inexplicable dream. He was in Boston, and I was in

New York, and yet I was ripped from my sleep by him screaming my name as if he were in the next room. I sat up and glanced in confusion at the clock: It was 3:15 in the morning. Eventually I went back to sleep, but I was awoken a few hours later by a phone call from my mother. She told me to get to Boston as fast as possible, because my father had tried to throw himself out of bed.

"Teo says he was trying to escape," my mother said. "That's a sign he's in his last few days."

Teo was a hospice nurse who had moved in with my parents. She was from Uganda and had attended scores of deaths. I asked my mother what time my father had done that, and I could hear her repeating the question to Teo.

"Three fifteen," my mother said.

When I got to Boston, I dragged a couch into my father's room so that I could sleep next to him. That night he woke up very agitated, and I held his hand and calmed him down until he drifted back to sleep. His rheumy blue eyes looked up at me like a young child's, full of love and relief. The next morning, my mother and I showed him photographs from his childhood. Spain in '36 before the fascists arrived. His stylish mother standing on the roof of a car during a street festival in Córdoba, the mayor of the city at her feet. His little sister, Renata, before the tragedy. His handsome, arrogant father with a cigarette tilted out of his lips.

At noon my father's oldest friend arrived, a Spanish woman named Teresa whom he had met in Paris after fleeing Spain. She sat holding his hand and watching him sleep. "On s'est bien aimé, eh, Miguel?" she said. "We really loved each other, didn't we?"

Teo kept pulling down the covers to check my father's feet.

"It has started," she announced around midday. I asked what she meant. "His toes are blue. They are not getting enough oxygen. Soon his feet will be blue, and then his legs. When the blue reaches his heart, he will die."

My father passed quietly in the early afternoon, and after the undertakers had carried him away, my mother and I drank Jerez in cut-glass green highballs that had been in the kitchen cabinets since I was a child. It was early April, and the sun was bright but had no warmth. The town had not yet swept up the sand and rock salt that accumulated over the winter, and the streets looked windy and grim. Teo took her leave, and that night I decided to sleep on the couch in my father's room one last time. His death bed was there, a hydraulic contraption with his body's shape still pressed into the mattress, and I caught myself having the odd thought that if any part of my father remained in the room, I didn't want him to be alone.

I lay down on the couch, but I couldn't sleep, so I sat back up and wrote down what I was thinking. *The price of getting to love somebody is having to lose them,* I wrote. *The price of getting to live is having to die.* I turned out the light and finally settled into a thin sleep, but suddenly my father was calling out to me again. This time he was coming from above, as if straight out of the night sky. I swung my legs off the couch and turned on the light, heart pounding; it was 3:15 in the morning.

The problem with rationality is that things keep happening that you can't explain, and I was never able to explain the dreams I had about my father. But maybe I didn't need to; maybe they're just the kind of coincidence that people love to find meaning in. My father was a devoted rationalist who nevertheless believed that humans have souls, and that each soul briefly exists as its own entity, like a wave on the ocean. Souls are made of something we don't understand yet, he said, and waves are just pulses of energy moving through a medium. My father believed that when we die, our souls are subsumed back into the vast soulmatter of the universe like waves subsumed back into the sea. He didn't believe in anything as simpleminded as heaven or as extravagant as reincarnation, but he also never looked up at the stars because he said he found the immensity overwhelming.

The first day I sat up and the second day I stood and the third day I walked. I was like a time-lapse film of child development. Very late on the second night, twenty-four hours after arriving in the ICU, I woke up in the beeping stillness with my heart rate at 120. I tried to deliberately calm my breathing but couldn't get the heart rate monitor to move; it was like I was running a race in my bed. I fought panic. What if my heart just couldn't keep up? What if I just ran out of air?

For some reason I was convinced that the breathing problems were my fault, so I shouldn't bother the nurses by calling them. There was a big red call button by my bed, but I thought of it as the "I give up" button rather than as the "I need help" button. I decided that if I made it to daybreak, I'd be okay. I watched the minute hand of the wall clock go ten minutes and then twenty. I felt like a fish stranded on the beach trying to breathe through its gills. Ten minutes later, I pushed the button. An athletic young man in a blue tracksuit came in to see what was wrong. I asked where he was from and he said, "Nigeria." I told him I'd been there a long time ago and that I couldn't breathe. He frowned and looked at the monitor and dialed my oxygen up to 5. Then he rushed out of the room.

When you receive a lot of blood or are in a car accident or suffer a severe impact, your chest cavity can fill with fluid and asphyxiate you by leaving your lungs no room to expand. Or you can get pneumonia—an infection and fluid buildup inside your lungs—and drown. There are many ways to die after a large blood transfusion, and a pulmonary crisis is one of the most common and rapid. The night nurse came back with a doctor who made a phone call and consulted with some other doctors and eventually a blood team came in. One of them had a bag of packed red blood cells between his hands like a big, raw steak. I lay on the bed, eyes wide and nostrils flaring like a quarter horse.

They transfused and sedated me, and I woke up the next morning to find Dr. Wilson at the foot of my bed. He put a stethoscope to my chest and told me to breathe and then talked to another man who seemed to be a technician and walked out of the room. Half an hour later, a young man came in pushing a portable chest x-ray. He scanned me and said I showed signs of collapsed lower lungs; untreated, that can lead to bacterial pneumonia and death. People die regularly in the ICU from mundane things like pneumonia after surviving extraordinary things like car accidents, gunshot wounds, and falls from great heights.

Fluid buildup is a constant threat, and some people become so bloated that their arms and legs look tiny in comparison to their bodies—"trauma toads," as they're known. I was put on intravenous antibiotics to prevent infection and diuretics to drain excess fluid, and by the next day, I could shuffle a full circle of the ICU, leaning on the rolling stand that held my IV and heart monitor. By day four I could do enough laps to start getting looks from the nurses, and the following morning I was released to the general ward. "Patient monitored with ICU care and eventually transferred to floor after incredible improvement," my chart noted. "Floor" referred to ordinary hospital rooms where patients are not thought to be in danger of dying.

I was discharged from the hospital after two days on the floor. The old athlete in me wanted to walk out, but the nurses insisted on a wheelchair until I got to the hospital entrance, at which point I could do whatever I wanted. It was a staggeringly hot day, and Barbara drove me through downtown Hyannis with the windows down and the air-conditioning on. I wanted to remember what the world smelled like. All I could think on the drive home was how long it would take to get me back to the hospital if I needed to. Would we turn around and make a dash for it or pull over and call an ambulance? For the first few exits it would make more sense to turn around, but eventually we would have to trust 911. I kept thinking that if the ambulance crew had been on a prior call a week ago, I'd have died. Ambulance crews can't put a Cordis line into your jugular or give you a blood transfusion; all they can do is give you a saline drip and drive faster.

An hour later we were home. The dirt driveway was thick with June heat and the puddles were baked dry. A bright piece of paper tacked to a tree read "BE HAPPY! We're waiting for you, so you should come home!" A few more drawings waited for me, and I was crying before I could get out of the car. Barbara led me inside the house and sat me on a bed. I'd made it.

Finding yourself alive after almost dying is not, as it turns out, the kind of party one might expect. You realize that you weren't returned to life, you were just introduced to death. Once I was blown up in a Humvee in Afghanistan and avoided injury because the bomb went off under the engine block instead of the crew compartment—a difference of about ten feet. I was jacked with adrenaline for the next few hours and then went careening into a depression that lasted days. I became paranoid about almost everything: where I sat, where I walked, what I sat behind. It was the ten feet that got me—the fact that "so much could be determined by so little," as I wrote in my notebook that night.

I was used to the idea that danger could kill me but not that my own body could; the fact that I was athletic and healthy should have been the end of the story. I had none of the things that typically drop middle-aged men in their tracks, and yet that's exactly what had happened. None of us are exempt. I know a young man who started having headaches. He got a brain scan, the doctors told him he was fine, but one neurologist happened to see the images and recommended more scans. That next round revealed a massive aneurysm that could kill him instantly. Surgeons rushed him into surgery and reached the aneurysm *as it started to rupture*. The doctor clamped it off and saved the young man's life. It was a matter of seconds.

The arbitrariness of death would seem to mean life has very little value unless you flip the equation upside down and realize that any existence with guarantees can be taken for granted far too easily. In a sense, modern society has the worst of both: lives that can end in a moment because that has always been true, but the illusion of guaranteed continuity. Biologically, I was supposed to die at fifty-eight from a ruptured pancreatic artery. My odds of surviving weren't Russian roulette odds—a comfortable 83.3 percent—or combat odds or even cancer odds. They were probably 10 or 20 percent by the time I finally got to the hospital and almost infinitely small before that because of the random details that determine who lives and who dies: whether I'd gone running that day, whether the ambulance was on a prior call, whether Dr. Dombrowski had already gone to bed. (You are statistically more likely to die at three in the morning than three in the afternoon because senior doctors try to avoid graveyard shifts. When one Manhattan radiologist did a follow-up on me, he incorrectly assumed my life had been saved during a daytime shift at NYU Langone. "You're lucky this didn't happen in the middle of the night," he said. "Or in Brooklyn.")

But I didn't die, and it made me wonder what this new part of my life was supposed to be called. The extra years that had been returned to me were too terrifying to be beautiful and too precious to be ordinary. A week after I came home, I found myself sitting at a window looking at a crab apple tree in the backyard. The branches were waving in the wind, and I had the thought that they'd be waving in exactly the same way if I'd died, only I wouldn't be here to see them. The moment would be utterly beyond my reach. Eventually Barbara asked if I felt lucky or unlucky to have almost died and I didn't know how to answer. Was I blessed by special knowledge or cursed by it? Would I ever function normally again?

The word *blessing* is derived from the Anglo-Saxon word

for blood—*bledsian*—and contains in its meaning the idea that there is no great blessing without sacrifice, and perhaps vice versa. The association may date to the ritual sacrifices of pre-Christian Europe as well as the hallowing of ground through combat. "We cannot dedicate—we cannot consecrate—we cannot hallow this ground," as Abraham Lincoln observed on the battlefields of Gettysburg in 1863. "The brave men, living and dead, who struggled here have consecrated it far above our poor power to add or detract." The ultimate struggle, of course, is with God. In Genesis, Jacob wrestles a man by the banks of a stream not knowing that his adversary is God Himself. At daybreak, God wearies of the contest and unjoints Jacob's hip by touching his thigh, but Jacob refuses to release him. "I will not let thee go except thou bless me," Jacob says.

God relents, and Jacob limps home blessed among men but crippled for life.

During a follow-up scan a year later, the radiologist spotted a five-centimeter mass against my pancreas. He called it a neoplasm, which is a medical term for new tissue that shouldn't be there. It was almost certainly a clump of old blood and scar tissue from the original bleed, but as one doctor said, "Just because you had a ruptured aneurysm doesn't mean you can't have pancreatic cancer." Pancreatic cancer is pretty much a death sentence, so I spent a summer undergoing one test after another. It's very easy to prove you have cancer, it turns out, and almost impossible to prove you don't. As test after test came back inconclusive, I sank into a kind of existential insanity. Every sunset, every dinner, every bedtime story dripped with ghastly significance because I might be dead in three months. Doctors came to seem like aloof priests who wielded fearsome power. Medical portals became thresholds to the great void. Do you want to know if you're going to live or die? Just log onto the hospital website and find out. Everything you ever wanted to know is waiting for you there. Waiting for us all.

Every day I cycled from an almost drugged state of appreciation to panic and back again. Barbara said she couldn't take much more of me like this and made the excellent point that I had an opportunity to experience the insights of terminal illness without—almost certainly—having to pay the price. What was I learning? What could I come away from this with? My father had continued reading history books until the last weeks of his life. Would I keep practicing music if the news were bad? Reading? Running? What would be the point—but then, what's the point anyway?

If the ultimate proof of God is existence itself—which many claim to be the case—then a true state of grace may mean dwelling so fully and completely in her present moment that you are still reading your books and singing your songs when the guards come for you at dawn. The past and the future have no tangible reality in our universe; God's creation exists moment by moment or not at all, and our only chance at immortality might lie in experiencing each of those moments as the stunning extravagance they actually are. But how is that even possible? Once in a bar in South Texas I saw a photograph of a Mexican rebel facing a firing squad. He stood in his old boots and peasant clothes with a cigar between his teeth and an expression of such calm superiority on his face that he made the men with the guns look like children. A day or an hour is just as precious to him as to us but we don't know that yet.

We will.

The closest I ever came to randomly getting killed wasn't in a war zone but directly in front of my apartment in New York City. I lived on Thirty-Sixth Street, just west of Eighth Avenue, in an old garment industry building. The cement floor still had bolt holes from the machinery. I was bicycling home one night and coasting to a stop, hands at my sides, when my front wheel caught a crack in the pavement and flipped sideways. Had I been going faster, the momentum would have carried me right through, but I was going walking pace. As I lunged to straighten the handlebars, I became aware of a car coming up very fast from behind—a gypsy cab accelerating to make the light. I managed to jam the handlebars back the other way and went over the top, piling headlong into the street. The car tires ripped past, inches from my head. I picked myself up, brushed the gravel out of my palms, and watched the cab's taillights hurtle off across Manhattan.

The story might have ended there, except that a few days later was when my friend Tim Hetherington was killed in Libya. It didn't take long for me to begin telling myself that I was the one who was supposed to die but had somehow given the universe the slip; it had been forced to take Tim instead.

A few days after coming home from the hospital in Hyannis, I was taking a shower when I realized that I finally had the answer to something I'd been wondering for years: What had Tim's last minutes been like? *The sky turned electric white, he shit his pants, and then he got sucked into a black pit*, I thought. Once again, I'd survived something he hadn't—another betrayal. Humans are pattern seekers, and now I had my pattern: When I live, someone else dies. Who was it going to be this time? My wife? My children? I leaned against the tile and cried until the shower ran cold.

Combat had never been this scary because it had never been this personal; there was just a lot of metal flying around, and you tried not to get in front of it. But now I was carrying my own destruction around with me like a live hand grenade. My understanding of median arcuate ligament syndrome was that a compression of the celiac artery forces blood into a bundle of much smaller pancreatic arteries, which dilate to accommodate the increased flow. One of the five arteries in my pancreas developed a weak spot and eventually ruptured from the pressure. After my discharge, I had asked Dr. Gorin if I had to fix the median arcuate ligament to live my full life.

"No," he said. "For some reason this never happens twice."

You don't have to be a physicist, though, to see that if you embolize one of the arteries leading to your pancreas, blood pressure is going to go up in the remaining four. It's the same amount of blood with 20 percent less vasculature. Despite what Gorin said, I became convinced that I was going to get another aneurysm, and I stopped going anywhere that was more than an hour from an interventional radiologist. That ruled out airplanes, traffic jams, walks in the woods, boat trips, foreign countries, even parts of this country. When I was alone in the house, I wrote down what was wrong with me on a piece of paper that I could hand to the EMTs or simply stuff into my shirt pocket in case I lost consciousness. Many times, I'd prepared myself for combat overseas in a similar way, arranging my boots and vest and camera and water and medical kit where I could find them fast in the dark; but in those situations, I was always surrounded by other men facing the same thing. Now I realized what an illusion that was. Even when we're with people we love, we are alone.

The flip side of terror is reverence; if you're not sufficiently reverent, you're not sufficiently terrified, and vice versa. My appreciation for the current moment rose to such levels that it could almost be paralyzing. There was virtually no activity that couldn't come grinding to a halt because I realized all over again how unlikely the whole thing was. *Why wasn't everyone crying all the time over this?* I thought. Have you seen the trees—really *seen* them? Or the clouds? Or the way water droplets form digital patterns on the porch screen after it rains? Religious people understand life is a miracle, but you don't need to sub it out to God to be rendered almost mute with wonder; just stand on a street corner and look around for a while.

Six months after the rupture, I had a consultation with Dr. Patrick Lamparello, a senior vascular surgeon at NYU Langone. Lamparello looked to be in his midseventies and said he had done some of the first laparoscopies forty years earlier in New York. I knew that there was a procedure where they could cut my median arcuate ligament, insert a stent inside the celiac, and allow the blood to flow through normally, and I wanted to know if I should do that to avoid another aneurysm. "Plus, I'm tired of worrying I could die at any moment," I added.

"Have you considered religion?" he said, so deadpan that I couldn't tell if he was joking. "Look, it's real surgery," he went on. "ICU afterwards, everything. And it might not work. Your problem is in the upper part of your abdomen, which is behind everything. You have to move all the organs just to get there. I've been in there many times; it's a big deal."

I saw a lot of doctors that summer, and I would always ask if any of their other patients had ever seen a dead relative while they were on the threshold. Not one doctor was willing to discuss it; in fact, the question invariably triggered the end of the visit. But my experience was common. I spent my recovery time reading through documentation gathered around the world of people who had almost died and remembered extremely strange things. Death had a rank and foul odor for me, as if a slavering beast was now breathing over my shoulder, and I thought that accounts of an afterlife might give me some kind of solace. At the very least, they might make me feel less alone. But then I would remember my dream. In many ways, the dream was worse than almost dying because it left me with the grotesque memory of being both conscious and dead at the same time. Not even the trauma bay had done that.

And the truth is that by the time you're actually dying, you're probably *not* going from your full beautiful life straight to oblivion; you're far more likely to be leaving a clutch of masked strangers speaking to each other in code while sticking tubes and needles into your body under very bright lights. Death is a huge distance to travel from a state of health and vigor, but if you're actually dying—and I have a distinct memory of this—you are already so compromised that it can just feel like a half step to the left.

The first person to systematically document and popularize near-death experiences was a philosopher and doctor named Raymond Moody, whose book *Life After Life* recounted numerous paranormal experiences. Moody was explicit in his belief in an afterlife, and that subjected him to accusations of cherry-picked data and confirmation bias. Following Moody, though, came a highly credentialed psychiatrist named Bruce Greyson. His book *After* starts with a single, startling anecdote: As an intern, Greyson rushed to the ER to assess a young woman who had nearly died of a drug overdose. As it so happened, he had just splattered spaghetti sauce on his tie while eating lunch, so he buttoned up his lab coat to cover it. The young woman's name was Holly. She was in a coma when Greyson arrived, but he was able to talk to Holly's roommate in the waiting room. The next day, after Holly woke up, she told Greyson two puzzling things: that she had "watched" his conversation with Susan and that he had a stain on his striped tie.

"The hair rose on the back of my neck, and I felt goose bumps," Greyson wrote. "For the past half century, I've been trying to understand how Holly could have known about the spaghetti stain."

Greyson went on to document more than one thousand near-death experiences—NDEs, as they came to be called. The central mystery, in medical terms, is how the dying brain could have such apparent clarity while suffering catastrophically low oxygen levels. More puzzling—or enticing—were anecdotes of the dying person seeming to have a kind of universal knowledge. How could Holly know about the spaghetti stain or see the conversation with her roommate if she was in a coma in another room? Another patient recalled traveling through the walls of the hospital to see her mother smoking in the waiting room, even though she had never known her mother to smoke. Yet another correctly said that a missing pair of dentures were in the drawer of a medical cart. This man had been brought to the hospital in a deep coma and had needed heart massage, defibrillation, and artificial respiration to survive.

"Oh, that nurse knows where my dentures are," he told a startled doctor, who wrote the encounter down. "You were there when I was brought into the hospital, and you took my dentures out of my mouth and put them in that cart, it had all these bottles on it and there was this sliding drawer underneath and there you put my teeth."

Greyson and later researchers, such as cardiologist Sam Parnia of Cornell University, went on to document the most common features of NDEs around the world. Parnia, in particular, was able to bring his expertise as a resuscitation specialist to bear on the puzzling gray zone between life and death. Parnia also tells a seminal story of a man whose heart stopped for almost an hour. Very sophisticated techniques allowed the man to survive without brain damage, and when he woke up four days later, he reported an extraordinary memory: he had been greeted by a "luminous, loving, compassionate being" that did not have "mass or a shape." He woke up without any fear of death.

I was finding it impossible not to root for an afterlife, and one of the things that triggered a flicker of optimism was the medical paradox of lucidity during collapsing brain function. The brain uses 15 percent of the oxygenated blood in the body and around 20 percent of the glucose. When the heart stops, those huge needs suddenly go unmet, and electrical activity in the brain plummets. And yet awareness seems to increase.

"The occurrence of lucid, well-structured thought processes together with reasoning, attention and memory recall of specific events during cardiac arrest (NDE) raise a number of interesting and perplexing questions," writes Parnia in the medical journal *Resuscitation*. "From a clinical point of view any acute alteration in cerebral physiology . . . leads to disorganized and compromised cerebral function."

Not only does the brain seem to continue functioning, it has experiences that are consistent across many, many cases. A study of near-death experiences around the world found *some* cultural variations—people from Anglo-European society were more likely to describe a journey through darkness as a "tunnel" rather than a "void"—but the basic contours of the experience were remarkably similar. The dying generally recall rising over their bodies, journeying to another realm, encountering dead relatives, and returning. A Māori woman named Nga, for example, recounted her brush with death to New Zealand author Michael King:

"I became seriously ill for the first time in my life," Nga said. "I became so ill that my spirit actually passed out of my body. My family believed I was dead because my breathing stopped . . . I had hovered over my head and then left the room and traveled northwards, towards the Tail of the Fish. I passed over the Waikato River, across the Manukau, over Ngāti Whātua, Ngāpuhi, Te Rarawa, and Te Aupōuri until I came to Te Rerenga Wairua, the leaping-off place of souls."

At that point, a voice told Nga to go back because it was not her time. She regained consciousness in her body, surrounded by family members.

In 1998, Dr. Greyson and two colleagues, Emily Cooke and Ian Stevenson, published a series of extraordinary accounts of near-death experiences in the *Journal of Scientific Exploration*. As explained in the abstract, they wanted to examine fourteen cases that, in their opinion, gave credence to the idea that individual consciousness survives death. Some cases were drawn from popular accounts published in newspapers, and some were from their own files. The researchers attempted to track down people from the accounts—sometimes decades later—and were able to confirm the stories in only the most general sense. It goes without saying that these are self-reported stories that, by definition, are impossible to confirm. The core experiences in the stories are remarkably consistent, though, and as I read them, I found it hard to imagine that deliberate falsifications would converge in such dramatic ways.

In every case cited by Greyson and his colleagues, the dying person found themselves outside their body and often looking down from above as doctors or bystanders tried to save them. Many also claimed to have perceptions that were not constrained by ordinary human perspectives. "In my wanderings there was a strange consciousness that I could see through the walls of the building," recorded a British army officer named Alexander Ogston, who almost died of typhoid fever at a military hospital around 1900. "I saw plainly, for instance, a poor Royal Army Medical surgeon, of whose existence I had not known, and who was in quite another part of the hospital, grow very ill and scream and die; I saw them cover his corpse and carry him softly out on shoeless feet, quietly and surreptitiously, lest we should know that he had died . . . Afterwards, when I told these happenings to the sisters [nurses], they informed me that all of this had happened."

According to Greyson and his colleagues, a nurse named Jean Morrow contacted them in 1991 to give her experience of almost dying in childbirth decades earlier: "Due to blood loss, my blood pressure dropped. When I heard, 'Oh my god, we're losing her,' I was out of body at once and on the ceiling of the operating room looking down—watching them work on a body."

Her account is similar to one given to Greyson by Peggy Raso, who barely survived a pulmonary embolism after giving birth to a healthy baby: "I, the real me, was not on the bed, and I began to think about this . . . I looked down at the bed from my vantage point near the ceiling. I saw a girl there who looked to be in a great deal of pain . . . I felt sorry for her. Doctors and nurses were coming and going from the room. I saw one doctor hit her hard on the chest. I tried to tell them I was not there. I saw a doctor come to the station that I recognized. He was a family friend and I had been raised next door to him. The nurse told him [Peggy Raso] had just died. He replied he would call Margaret (my mother). My hearing was extremely acute. I heard and saw another patient on the floor complaining about the activity and noise coming from my room. It dawned on me they were talking about me. I tried to tell them I was not down there. It became obvious they were not hearing me."

Another recurring theme in many near-death experiences is encountering dead loved ones and other spirits. Not only have researchers documented this from around the world, but virtually every society believes that when you die, you will be reunited with loved ones who have already passed. This belief exists in the entire spectrum of human society, from small-band hunter-gatherers to mass industrialists, and forms a core part of almost all religions, including Christianity. In fact, to be Christian is to take the resurrection of Christ literally. From 1 Corinthians 15: "If there is no resurrection of the dead, then not even Christ has been raised. And if Christ has not been raised, then . . . your faith is futile, and you are still in your sins."

Around one quarter of near-death survivors report encountering the dead, as I did. Some were long-dead relatives, some were the recently dead, and some were not yet known to have died. One American soldier responded to an appeal in military publications for near-death experiences with this account of a helicopter crash in Vietnam: "It was peaceful and cool. I could see others like myself just sort of floating around only inches from the ground . . . dead [Viet Cong]. Our eyes meet, but there are no hard feelings between us, just something we have in common . . . people walk past you, and you know what they are thinking . . . we all have the same thing in common . . . we are dead."

On the face of it, arguing there is no "afterlife" is not a particularly winning idea, so skeptics tend to publish research papers rather than bestselling books. These papers are written in dense medical language that seems intended for other scientists rather than the reading public, and the conclusions are always mild mannered but unequivocal: there is no rational reason to believe that NDEs are anything but hallucinations. The brain is by far the most complex structure in the known universe, with an estimated hundred trillion neural connections, and those connections give rise to an extremely mysterious phenomenon called consciousness. Consciousness is still far beyond the capability of the largest computer networks but extremely vulnerable to distortion. Hallucinations, visions, disembodied voices, premonitions, and visions of God can feel extremely real but have no provable basis in reality.

Neurophysiologist Christof Koch questions life reviews in simple biological terms: "Your EEG goes flat and then you have these experiences? I've never seen data to that effect," he told me. "I'm extremely skeptical. You get cardiac arrest, your heart stops. Everyone is frantic and injects you with sedatives, they shock your heart, and sometime later you wake up in a hospital bed. How do you know when exactly the experience happened with the EEG? Everything we know from the last 120 years of studying the brain, when your EEG is flat, when there's no electrical activity, there's no consciousness in your brain."

And yet, Koch almost died and remembers an ecstatic experience with a brilliant light. "I lost everything. I lost my body, the world, my ego. There was no more Christof, there was just bright light, ecstasy. And it stays with you. Every day, I think about it. You lose borders between yourself and others. Right now, in normal conditions, I know this pen is not part of my body; I've learned there are borders between me and the rest of the world. So even if you make love to your wife and your bodies are intertwined, you still know, *This is my leg and this is her leg*. But under special circumstances, you can lose these borders and feel you are part of everything. Some people argue that this is evidence of universal consciousness. It's quite possible. I think it's *unlikely*, but I cannot rule it out on logical grounds."

For NDE believers, the ultimate refutation of Koch's gentle

skepticism is the case of a thirty-five-year-old musician named Pam Reynolds. In 1991, Reynolds was diagnosed with a basilar artery aneurysm so deep in her brain that surgeons could not access it with conventional means. It was a death sentence, so surgeons resorted to a rare and high-risk procedure called hypothermic cardiac arrest. The plan was to lower her body temperature to 50 degrees Fahrenheit to prevent tissue decay, stop her heartbeat and breathing, drain the blood from her head, saw open her skull, excavate her brain to the depth of the aneurysm, repair the artery so that it would not rupture, and then reverse the process until Reynold's heart could be jump-started with a defibrillator.

Reynolds was given general anesthesia, her eyes were taped shut, and Dr. Robert Spetzler started his bone saw and cut a section out of her skull. A surgical microscope was inserted deep into her brain, to the site of the aneurysm. Her heart was stopped, her body was chilled, and the blood was drained from her head by gravity. At that point, all brain waves ceased, and her EEG went flat.

The operation was a success, but after Reynolds woke up in the ICU, she had the strangest things to report. She said that despite the general anesthesia, she was brought back to awareness by the sound of the cranial saw, and that she had then slipped out the top of her head and looked down from the surgeon's shoulder. At some point she overheard a conversation between doctors about trying to establish a vascular entry point in her groin, which surprised her, because she knew that the surgery was nowhere near that area. Later she encountered dead relatives, including her uncle, who urged her to slip back into her mangled body. She saw her body "jump" twice—supposedly the two defibrillator shocks—and later found herself returning to consciousness in the recovery room.

According to Reynolds's anesthesiologist, however, there is no way to know at what point Reynolds had her experiences. If her brain had zero blood perfusion and her EEG was flat, it is medically impossible for her to have any thoughts or memories. Far more likely, in their view, is the possibility that her memories came from a period of semiconsciousness before and after anesthesia, during which she might have overheard the surgical team discussing the details of her surgery.

The Reynolds case is unique, though; far more common are NDEs where the brain keeps functioning even though the heart has stopped, and there is every reason to think that a person who survives that might have strange memories. Depriving the brain of oxygen is known to cause cognitive distortions, tunnel vision, loss of consciousness, and an accompanying phenomenon, the buildup of carbon dioxide in the blood stream, is thought to trigger release of a psychedelic compound called DMT (N,N-Dimethyltryptamine). The drug is chemically related to ayahuasca, the powerful "death vine" used by indigenous shamans in the Amazon basin, and it occurs naturally in spinal fluid. Endogenous DMT, as it is known, protects neurons from cell death during episodes of low oxygen or high carbon dioxide, which would make it a natural fit for near-death experiences.

The rejoinder to the "dying brain" hypothesis is that people falling from great heights or about to have a car crash do not have low blood oxygen or high carbon dioxide levels, and yet they often have life reviews, visions, and other classic near-death experiences. And people struggling with oxygen supply, such as asthma sufferers, do not generally entertain visions of the dead or have spiritual epiphanies. But psychological stress is also known to flood the brain with powerful neurochemicals that can cause hallucinations and feelings of ecstasy and removal. One researcher compared first-person descriptions of hundreds of near-death experiences with fifteen thousand drug trips and found a very close match between NDEs and a synthetic drug called ketamine.

"The experience I had on ketamine was like a near-death experience, and it was terrifying," one psychologist told me. "I felt like I was being pulled deeper and deeper into nothingness. I was almost stitched into the fabric of something. The therapist that was with me said that I said two things during that time. One was, *Am I just supposed to die?* And, *Am I ever going to see my kids again?*"

Ketamine is an opioid that is also thought to occur naturally in the human body. When lab animals are subjected to a terrifying attack—an experiment that can't be duplicated with people, obviously—their brains are flooded with dopamine and other opioids. Artificial ketamine is already known to protect cells destroyed by low blood oxygen in brain injury victims, and an endogenous version manufactured inside the body that accomplishes the same thing would make biological sense. The hallucinations and euphoria that accompany these compounds could provide an additional evolutionary benefit by helping calm and reassure the person whose survival is on the line.

Harvard endocrinologist Daniel Carr refers to these stress reactions as limbic lobe syndrome. The limbic system is involved

in emotional processing, long-term memory, and survival be-
haviors. It includes the hippocampus and the amygdala, which
process memories, decisions, and basic emotions such as fear and
aggression. According to Carr, the limbic system contains a dis-
proportionate number of opioid receptors as well as high levels
of the endogenous opioids themselves.

A final explanation for NDEs involves temporal lobe seizures, which doctors have triggered by implanting electrodes
in the cortex of epilepsy patients as part of a mapping process
before surgery. (Because the brain cannot feel pain, patients are
kept conscious to report what they are experiencing.) A Canadian neurologist named Wilder Penfield pioneered this technique in the 1950s, demonstrating how electrical stimulation to
different areas of the brain can trigger intense memories, out-of-
body experiences, déjà vu, and a feeling of euphoria or dread—
all common symptoms of NDEs. When Penfield stimulated one
young epileptic at a depth of two centimeters into his temporal
lobe, he shouted, "Oh God, I'm leaving my body!" Another, fe-
male patient reported a strange sensation, "As if I am not here. As
though I were half [there] and half here."

The fact that NDEs resemble temporal lobe seizures does not
mean they cause them, but the stress of impending death might
trigger a response in the hippocampus that facilitates the absorp-
tion of endogenous compounds like ketamine, which is known
for its calming effects and ephemeral experiences. "The hippocampus is the central processing area of the brain and . . . most
associated with consciousness and the soul," one team noted.
"Such genetically determined areas . . . may well serve as a natural

defense mechanism against stressful situations such as childbirth and trauma. This would also explain how certain religions use control of the autonomic nervous system to produce out-of-body states and religious ecstasy."

Humans evolved from their primate origins as mobile hunter-gatherers who depended on increasingly complex understandings of existence to survive and thrive. And part of that survival was psychological: we had to hold a sense of our own unique selves alongside the foreknowledge of our mortality. One solution to this brutal cognitive dissonance was to believe that the boundary between life and death was blurry and that our apparent individuality was part of the warp and weft of existence. Souls are liberated from the body at death, spirits can move unconstrained by time and space, and the dead can drift through walls and rattle doorknobs. When I was in my midthirties, I had a dream that I left my body and rushed through the night sky. When I woke up, I wrote the following in my notebook:

"I am moving through the dark house, and I am outside and moving across the land. Naked and so gray I'm invisible and vibrating with power, moving impossibly slowly and fast at the same time, every breath a lifetime, existing so heavily in the here-and-now that reality could burst at the seams and come spilling out as a liquid known as time."

The question isn't whether such dreams represent objective reality—they obviously don't—but why people keep having them. The world over, people believe in two realities: one we walk around in and the "other" that we go to from time to time. Drugs, dreams, religion, and death are the ways people are generally thought to cross over. My dream was indistinguishable from both an NDE and a "shamanic journey" of the sort that anthropologists have documented from tribal cultures across the globe. Shamanism is a paleolithic-era practice that survived long enough for ethnographers to document in places as varied as the Siberian tundra, the Amazon jungle, the arctic ice fields, the African rain forests, and the canyons and uplands of central Mexico. It is one of the few human universals. The shaman flies his body and becomes a spirit, traveling to the land of the dead and returning with knowledge that is needed by the community. Hallucinogens, drumming, fasting, and hours or even days of dancing help the shaman leave this reality and reach the next.

An annihilating vision of the cosmos has been central to the human experience for tens of thousands of years, and human beings have long used drugs to find a meaningful place in it. Archeologists at the Es Càrritx cave in Mallorca, Spain, have found three-thousand-year-old locks of hair preserved in ceremonial wood and horn containers. The hair was found to have high levels of the hallucinogens atropine, scopolamine, and ephedrine. All three drugs can be derived from plants native to Mallorca, particularly *Datura stramonium*, also known as jimsonweed.

But in addition to the drug use, archeologists noticed an odd pattern of circles carved into the wood and horn vessels. Neolithic Mallorcans depended on plants and animals to survive, yet they decorated their most sacred objects with simple concentric rings. Similar rings have appeared in ceremonial objects around the world, and scholars equate them with a kind of "inner vision" associated with hallucinogens. Ancient ceramic containers from

Arkansas have identical designs carved in them—and have also tested positive for atropine. Clearly, people around the world have been seeking the same thing.

It was hard not to wonder what my father would make of all this. Would he propose some kind of cosmic theory to explain how he came to be floating above me in the trauma bay, or would he write the whole thing off to neurochemicals and wishful thinking? The idea that physical existence has no other enduring dimension might one day seem as incomprehensible as the earth being flat or could wind up being the most fundamental of all the physical laws that we understand.

I invited two former colleagues of my father's for lunch to talk about it, Rudolph Martinez and Joel Garrelick. They had worked with my father for years on something called the Helmholtz resonator, which is a cavity with specific acoustical properties. When you blow across the top of a bottle and produce a whistling sound, you have just created a Helmholtz resonator. Joel and Rudolph knew my father extremely well and had many times watched his strange, brilliant mind work through a problem. I told them how he had appeared above me in the trauma bay and asked what they thought he might have said about it.

"Your father was a romantic, and as such, he wouldn't be averse to considering any such thing," Rudolph said. "He was a great scientist. Rational to the hilt, of course, but he was also a romantic."

That surprised me—and certainly would have surprised my mother. When she and my father decided to elope, he suggested San Francisco, and she was delighted until she realized that he also wanted to catch the annual meeting of the Acoustical Society of America.

"He was a romantic because he was deeply in love with the Helmholtz resonator," Rudolph added. "Countless comments and examples about the Helmholtz."

I asked if there could be a dimension where time does not exist, and my father could be both alive and dead—and therefore able to visit me.

"Yes, there is. All you have to do is travel at the speed of light and time stops. A second becomes eons—but as perceived by somebody else. For you, a second is a second."

"The big bang is an issue," Joel added. "But I don't think Miguel would have gone there. You said you didn't know you were in danger of dying, right?"

"Right," I answered.

"So, I think he would have taken that as a sign that there is something physical," Joel said. "Something is happening in your body, so your body knows you're dying. Something is prompting some electrical circuit to do something in your memory."

I asked what I thought was an impossible question: What are the odds that my father would appear above me as I died? To my surprise, Rudolph looked upwards for a moment and seemed to be running some numbers.

"Like, ten to the minus sixty," he said.

"Ten to the minus sixty?"

Rudolph explained that the odds of my father materializing in a corner of the room were roughly the same as all the oxygen molecules suddenly winding up in one corner and asphyxiating us. "It's about the number of molecules in any volume, like a cubic meter—ten to the twenty-third power," he said. "Actually, it's 6.03

times ten to the twenty-third power. It's called Avogadro's number. Anything is possible: Jesus could have walked on water."

"It's just very unlikely," added Joel.

Doctors approach near-death experiences very much like my father approached physics, and they have come up with prosaic explanations for just about everything. Tunnels, bright lights, life reviews, Godheads, out-of-body experiences, feelings of peace and unity, cosmic insight, and a disinterest in the corporeal world can all be induced in people fairly easily—and happen all the time. You don't need to believe in an afterlife to explain the visions of a hypoxic brain or the out-of-body illusions of someone suffering a seizure.

With one central exception: the dead.

Why do the dying—and *only* the dying—keep seeing the dead in their last days and hours? If there is any true mystery to all this, it's that in mud huts and in hospital rooms, in car accidents and on battlefields, in darkened bedrooms and in screaming ambulances, deathly ill people are startled to see a loved one hovering over them. There are neurochemical explanations for why people hallucinate, but not for why they keep hallucinating the same thing. Some attempts have been made, though: the visions are said to be unconscious projections ginned up by terrified patients, or evolutionary adaptations that aid survival, or simply cultural expectations that are expressed in imaginary form. Those proposals fall well short of explaining the broad and powerful sweep of this phenomenon across the world.

One of the most notable aspects of these visions is how startled the dying seem to be. I was deeply shocked to see my father and in no way comforted by him; in fact, I was mortified. Hours before dying, my mother squinted at a corner of the bedroom and said, "What's *he* doing here?" I guessed it was her estranged brother, George, long dead of throat cancer.

"That's George," I said. "He's come a long way to see you, and you have to be nice to him."

"We'll see about that," she said.

After Tyler Carroll left the military, he took a job as a paramedic for a fire department. One day he picked up a seventy-year-old woman who was having trouble breathing. He put a twelve-lead on her and determined that she was having a heart attack, so he loaded her into the ambulance for a trip to the hospital. Five minutes later she sat bolt upright, as if she'd seen something, and said in amazement, "I'm about to die." Then she lay back and died.

One wonders what she saw. Because of the prevalence of sedation, the dying are not always clear-minded, but occasionally someone makes it to their last breath without morphine. One nurse told me that she took care of a man who was pain-free until the very end and entirely lucid. Hours before he died, she heard him say the name "Barbara" over and over, as if she were present in the room. The nurse went into the kitchen to tell the man's wife.

"Barbara was the love of his life," the woman said, crying. "She was our nineteen-year-old."

To the extent that the historical record can be trusted, there are scores of cases from previous centuries as well. Many were collected by a British physicist named William F. Barrett and published posthumously as a short volume called *Deathbed Visions*.

Barrett was born in Jamaica in 1844 to missionary parents who ran an underground waystation for escaped slaves. He studied physics and chemistry before moving on to occult topics such as telepathy and hypnotism—for which he was roundly mocked. But his book on deathbed visions became a classic compendium of something that many people recognized but no one understood. Barrett claims he did his best to confirm the details of the stories, but obviously that was not even possible then—much less now. That said, the accounts are startlingly consistent not only with each other but with many accounts from today.

In Barrett's era, people tended to die at home, unmedicated, often with siblings or friends having preceded them. Death was common and familiar to most people and not necessarily something to be feared. Over and over, the people described in Barrett's book were startled to see deceased relatives in the room and usually felt calmed by them, even delighted. "Marion, my daughter!" one man shouted shortly before he died. Some encounters even felt like a family reunion: "Look, there they all are, William and Elizabeth and Emma and Anne—and Priscilla too!" one woman exclaimed after waking from a coma. (William was a son who had died many years earlier in infancy; Priscilla was a family friend who had passed away two days prior.)

In an era of slow communication, it was entirely possible to not know that a close friend or even family member had died, and Barrett considered visits by the recently dead to be exceptionally strong evidence of an afterlife. A Frenchman named Paul Durocq died of yellow fever while traveling with his family in Venezuela, in 1894. In his last hours, he seemed to be visited by the spirit of a close friend who had died while the Durocqs were away—although they didn't know that. The Durocqs found his funeral announcement in the mail when they got home.

Barrett also considered the death visions of children to be particularly persuasive. "On Nov 2nd and 3rd, 1870, I lost my two eldest boys, David and Harry, to scarlet fever, they being three and four years old, respectively," one man told Barrett. "Harry died at Abbott's Langley on November 2nd, fourteen miles from my vicarage at Aspley; David the following day at Aspley. About an hour before the death of this latter child, he sat up in bed, and pointing to the bottom of the bed said distinctly, 'There is little Harry calling me.'"

The overwhelming likelihood is that our sense of another reality is just a comforting illusion that helps us live our lives. But what appears to be likely or unlikely is a terrible strategy for finding out what is true. Our understanding of reality might be as limited as a dog's understanding of television. So, abandoning likelihood for a moment, one might try out the idea that death is simply where the veil of belief gets rent to reveal a greater system beyond. "Reality" may just be a boundary we can't see past. The dead might be all around, flitting back and forth as the dying take their leave. Imagine their frantic efforts around floods and earthquakes. Around epidemics. Around Dachau.

It's not remotely likely, but then neither is anything. If the force of gravity were even slightly weaker, stars wouldn't be dense enough to cross the Coulomb barrier and start thermonuclear fusion. It would be a completely dark universe. If gravity were slightly stronger, stars would burn too hot and fast, and there would be no life. If the attractive force between electrons and atomic nuclei were too weak, electrons couldn't orbit; if it were too strong, atoms couldn't bond with each other. Either way, there would be no molecules. There are more than thirty such parameters that must have almost the precise values that they do in order to permit a universe with life. The odds of that happening have been calculated to be one to the negative 230—that is to say, one chance in a number that has 229 zeros after it. Randomly finding a specific grain of sand on the first try among all the grains on earth would be millions of millions of times more likely than the universe existing. And yet here we are.

Given that existence itself is almost infinitely unlikely, what *if* there were some kind of post-death existence? What *if* the dead were not entirely gone, in the sense that we understand that word, and the living were not entirely bound by time and space? What *if* the great mysteries of the world—the spirits and ghosts and coincidences and telepathy and predictive dreams and everything else that humans have always noticed but couldn't quite make sense of—actually had a rational explanation?

How would that possibly work?

In the basest terms, death is a final spike in the entropy that all living creatures must fight in order to exist. Entropy is another word for disorder. A boulder on a hill is a favored analogy: One push and it rolls to the bottom, where it loses all its kinetic energy until some force—such as a bulldozer—pushes it back to the top. It takes a lot more energy to push a boulder to the top of a hill than to start rolling it down, but once it's at the top, one could say that the energy has been "stored" against gravity for future use.

At every scale, the universe has suffered a net loss of stored energy since the big bang. More stars are collapsing than are being born, more gas molecules are spreading out than are coming together, more heat is dispersing than is being generated. Eventually the universe will cool to a temperature so close to absolute zero that there will be no light, no thermal energy, no atomic movement and therefore no time. The cosmos does not go howling on forever, in other words; it is born, ages, and dies like we do. When people hope for eternal life, they are hoping for something that even the universe, fourteen billion light-years across and still expanding at the speed of light, cannot be granted.

But humans can delay entropy for a little while—a lifetime, in fact—by eating food, drinking water, and breathing air. We are the metabolic equivalent of a person pushing a boulder up a hill. When we eat grains or vegetables, we are eating something that got its energy from the sun; when we eat meat, we are eating something that got its energy from plants that, in turn, got their energy from the sun. Food can be thought of as stored sunlight, and sunlight can be thought of as stored energy from the big bang. When we die, we stop being able to metabolize food, and the cellular barriers that separate us from the outside world break down. The boulder rolls back to the bottom of the hill.

Entropy-defying patterns are not limited to the biological world. A bathtub full of water is without internal order—a high-entropy state—until you open the drain, at which point energy in the form of gravity creates a vortex of water rushing out to reestablish equilibrium. No individual water molecules persist in the vortex because they are swept down the drain, but taken together, they create an extremely stable structure that continues so long as the drain is open and there is water in the tub. As chemist Addy Pross points out, all human cells are replaced many times over but maintain a pattern—the human body—that persists as long as those cells can metabolize energy. And all those human bodies, in turn, constitute the species *Homo sapiens sapiens* that persists across generations even though the individuals that make up the human race keep dying. (Or, as Xana put it: "Daddy, I know why there is night. So other people can have day.")

One could say that when my aneurysm burst on June 16, 2020, order started rushing out of me and entropy started rushing in. Throughout history and across societies, moral behavior usually boils down to not treating people as if they are disposable—perhaps because we intuitively know that entropy will make that clear soon enough. Any theory of an afterlife would have to explain how souls can survive an end-state universe of –459.67 degrees Fahrenheit, otherwise known as absolute zero. One would have to imagine a zero-energy state for souls, which is another way of saying that they don't exist. "The universe of energy is, we are told, running down," neuroscientist Sir Charles Sherrington observed sadly. "It tends fatally towards equilibrium. An equilibrium in which life cannot exist. If mind is not an energy system, how will the running down of the universe affect it? Can it go unscathed? Will the universe—which elaborated and is elaborating the finite mind—let it perish?"

In fact, the physics of Sherrington's day had begun to demonstrate quite the opposite: matter was ultimately dependent on human consciousness rather than the other way around. It was a deeply counterintuitive reversal that got its start in 1900, when a moderately promising German physicist named Max Planck decided to solve an arcane but stubborn problem involving thermal radiation, the energy given off by hot bodies. In a single evening, Planck invented the "quantum of action." A quantum is the smallest possible unit of energy that can be given off by an electron, and Planck showed that energy is radiated in units rather than waves. In the macroscopic world, when a pendulum swings, it does not "jump" from one position to another; it moves in a smooth and continuous way. At the subatomic level, however, electrons are either "here" or "there," but never in between. They do not swing, in other words; they leap. The formula that predicts how electrons leap from one energy level to another is called Planck's constant and is considered one of the basic laws of nature, along with gravity and the speed of light.

Planck's law constituted a new kind of knowledge that was demonstrably true despite the fact that even its discoverers didn't quite understand it. Einstein supposedly said that Paul Dirac's breakthrough on antimatter bordered on insanity; Richard Feynman supposedly declared that if you think you understand quantum mechanics, you don't understand quantum mechanics. On some level, the central tenets of quantum mechanics had to be taken on faith, like a new kind of religion—the crucial difference being that science stands ready to be disproven by facts, whereas religion does not. Followed to its logical conclusion, the Planck constant meant that the laws of physics governing the macroscopic world—planets, pool balls, pendulums—fail at the subatomic level. A different set of laws take over that seem to defy not only common sense but everything that was previously known.

Planck's breakthrough led Albert Einstein, working daytimes in a government patent office, to propose that light was composed of quantum packets that could behave either like particles *or* like waves. None of these phenomena were visible, but the mathematics that describe them have no alternative. Einstein's work allowed Niels Bohr to calculate the angular momentum of an electron, which helped Louis de Broglie demonstrate that electrons circling a nucleus behave like waves as well as little planets. This was named the wave-particle duality, and after Einstein studied it, he said that de Broglie had "lifted a corner of the veil that shrouds the Old One."

Nothing in the observable world could be in two places at once—it made no sense—and yet at the subatomic level, that's exactly what seemed to be happening. It was as if you could prove a schizophrenic delusion with math. Then, over the course of one day and one night, while on vacation at a seaside resort, Werner Heisenberg discovered matrix quantum mechanics. He was twenty-three years old. Heisenberg's theory proposed that an electron is not a particle that exists at one place at one time the way a person or a chair does; rather, it occupies all positions at once as a statistical probability. When you pin it down by observing it with a detector, the electron freezes in place, and you lose all information about its momentum. When you stop observing it, you regain information about its momentum but lose its location. There was no way to have both.

That paradox famously came to be known as the Heisenberg uncertainty principle and forced physicists to come to the impossible conclusion that the subatomic world was *brought into existence* by observation. The act of observing something created the very thing that was being observed—which, until then, had existed only as a set of probabilities called a wave function. Theoretically, Schrödinger's cat was a massive wave function—both alive and dead—until the box was opened, at which point its wave function collapsed into one outcome or the other. That was happening to all matter all the time, creating the world we live in.

These were not mathematical games that worked only on paper; they were real-world phenomena that quantum theory could predict to an estimated accuracy of one millionth of a percent. When a photon is fired at two slits, it passes through *both* as a probability until it is tracked by a photon detector, in which case its wave function collapses, and it picks just one. Stranger still, some particles were also found to be "entangled" at the quantum level, so that if you did something to one, its twin reacted as well. Unlike what was possible in the macroscopic world, the change was instantaneous and unaffected by distance. That forced a choice: Either quantum information can travel faster than light, or particles have what Einstein called "hidden variables" that determine their future behavior. Neither is possible in the universe we know.

The experiments unnerved even the men who were conducting them. Einstein was so troubled by the implications of Bohr's theories that he tried to refute them but wound up having to violate his own theory of relativity to do so. Schrödinger resorted to quoting the Vedic Upanishads, which maintain that there is an ultimate universal reality, called *Brahman*, and an inner consciousness, called *Atman*, and that they are the same thing. Sir Arthur Eddington—who helped prove Einstein's general theory of relativity during the solar eclipse of 1919—simply observed, "Something unknown is doing we don't know what."

But what is true at the subatomic level can also be true for the entire universe. Physicists eventually proposed that the universe existed as a nearly infinite wave function containing all possible outcomes until conscious thought forced it to spring into existence in its current singular form. Oddly, the idea had a distant religious origin from the early 1600s, when a lapsed Polish Jesuit named Casimir Liszinski wrote a secret treatise proposing that it was humans who created God rather than the other way around. Unfortunately, Liszinki had lent a large sum of money to a neighbor named John Brzoska, and Brzoska came up with a plan to avoid paying back the debt. He stole Lisinski's manuscript and turned it over to church authorities, who quickly stood Liszinski before a tribunal and condemned him to death. His treatise was destroyed but, ironically, its main points were preserved when they were read into the court records. They include the following (slightly edited for brevity):

> We beseech you . . . do you not extinguish the light of Reason, do you not oust the sun from this world, do you not pull down your God from the sky, when attributing to him the impossible. Man is the creator of God, and God

is a concept and creation of Man. God is not existent. Piety
was introduced by the impious. The fear of God was spread
by the unafraid so that the people would be afraid of them
in the end. Simple folk are cheated by the more cunning
with the fabrication of God for their own oppression.

In religious terms, Liszinski's crime was heresy—the contra-
dicting of God's word. Heresy comes from the classical Greek
word *haireomai*, "to choose," and has long been one of humani-
ty's most savagely punished crimes. As the bishop of Kyiv noted
with satisfaction, Liszinski was to have his tongue torn out with
red-hot tongs for having offended God, his hands roasted slowly
at a fire for having written against God, his manuscript burned
before his eyes for having offended God, and then he was to be
burned alive and his ashes shot out of a cannon. The punishment
was cruel even by church standards of the day, and a royal com-
mutation reduced it to mere "beheading and burning."

Liszinski's plea was that not only do you deprive God of dig-
nity by insisting He be something He can't—self-creating—but
you also strip society of the benefits of reason. There is a point at
which reason fails, however. The entire universe can be understood
mathematically to the subatomic level, but only religion claims to
know how it came to exist in the first place. Math and reason fail utterly in this regard. Without God, either existence is inevitable—a
state for which there are no mathematics—or it is *almost* infinitely
unlikely but came into existence during an infinity of time.

When I was young, my father told me stories about people

like Liszinski who were martyred for insisting on logic and reason. Without these people, he said, there would be no medicine,
no advanced technology, no structural engineering, no math, no
science, and no philosophy. According to him, the reason Arab
society was more advanced than European society in the Middle
Ages was because the Caliphate made sure to protect Arab scholars from the retrograde effects of religion. He would regularly re-
cite all the scientific words that begin with "al"—alchemy, algebra,
alcohol, Aldebaran—to make sure I knew they came from a sec-
ular Arab study of the world. That ended during the Age of Enlightenment, when Europe turned to science and reason to explain
reality while the Arab world slid into autocratic theology. The two
societies flipped roles, and my father insisted that Arab society has
still not recovered from the social and economic consequences of
attributing everything to God.

One evening when my parents were first married, my mother
was cooking dinner when she heard my father muttering to himself,
"That's so beautiful. That's the most gorgeous thing I've ever seen."
My father was sitting in an armchair with a book open on his lap,
and my mother tiptoed over to see what form of beauty had so captured her new husband's eye. He was reading a physics book, and the
page was entirely covered in equations and numbers. My father was
working for the US Navy at the time, trying to make navy propellers
quieter, and I have a photograph of him and twenty other scientists
seated at conference tables in a huge semicircle. They were all men,
all of them were taking notes, and half were smoking. In my father's
handwriting on the back it says "Quiet Torpedo Meeting July 1976."

I survived my aneurysm because scientists very much like my father developed nearly miraculous procedures for keeping people alive. And then he appeared above me at the worst—and almost the last—moment of my life in a form that he and every man at the Quiet Torpedo Meeting would surely have dismissed as a hallucination. Now I find myself reading papers on quantum theory and cosmology, trying to understand what I saw; trying to understand why he was there. He appeared when I needed him most. It was quite possibly his greatest act of love toward me. He was a distracted and distant father, a germophobe who hesitated to pick up his own children and could disappear into his thoughts for hours at a time—and yet there he was. *It's okay, you don't have to fight it. I'll take care of you. You can come with me.*

I wouldn't mind if he hovered above me on the couch from time to time to explain these physics papers to me. The ideas in them were produced by a kind of high-functioning derangement on the part of the physicists—you can't invent quantum of action in a single evening in an ordinary state of mind—and honestly, they are making me a little crazy as well. Not only is the language almost nonsensical in its density and precision, it utterly destroys our shared sense of reality.

We assume that life is the most real thing we will ever experience, but it might turn out to be the least real, the least meaningful. The idea that you will appreciate life more after almost dying is a cheap bit of wisdom easily asserted by people who have never been near death. When you drill down into it—which you must—we are really talking about an appreciation of death rather than of life. Eventually you will be all alone with doctors shrugging because they've run out of things to do, and the person you *really* are thumping frantically in your chest: the successes and catastrophes and affairs and hangovers and genuine loves and small betrayals and flashes of courage and the river of fear running beneath it all, and of course the vast stretches of wasted time that are part of even the most amazing life.

You will know yourself best at that moment; you will be at your most real, your most honest, your most uncalculated. If you could travel back in time to make use of such knowledge during your life, you would become exactly the person you'd always hoped to be—but none of us do that. We don't get that knowledge until it's too late because then it can't be tainted by vanity or pride or desire.

I f you raise children without religion, you are raising children who will ask questions you cannot answer. If a child asks religious parents where the universe comes from, the answer is invariably "God," but those parents will have fallen for the "first cause" fallacy: if everything has a creator, then God must, too, in which case you are right back where you started. (Physicists can't answer such questions either, but their profession is based on acknowledging that.)

"With the expansion of science, it becomes more and more complicated to talk about God in simplistic terms," writes Stanford physicist Andrei Linde. "Apparently, the laws of the universe work so precisely that we do not need any hypothesis of a divine intervention in order to describe the behavior of the universe as we know it. There remained one point which was hidden from us and which remained unexplained: the moment of creation of the universe as a whole. The mystery of creation of everything from nothing could seem too great to be considered scientifically."

When I was young, I asked my father how the universe came

into existence, and he said that he was not smart enough to understand it, but that some people were. "I'm not even smart enough to understand the theory of relativity," he added. My father was referring to cosmologists who had figured out how to look back in time by studying the distant edges of the universe. By measuring radiation left over from what is known as the big bang, they have reverse-engineered the process to pinpoint the moment of creation at 13.787 billion years ago, plus or minus about .15 of a percent of the total. At that point, the universe theoretically measured one "Planck length"—the smallest possible distance of the subatomic world—and was infinitely hot and dense. This is referred to as the "singularity" and is as close as physicists come to talking about God.

At the theoretical singularity there was no time, no light, no space, no gravity, no mathematics, no laws of physics, and no constants; every value was infinite. Science writer Jim Holt has described it as a "closed space-time of zero radius," meaning that it contained the three dimensions of space and the one dimension of time within an infinitely small point. But Heisenberg's uncertainty principle says that every state—even nothingness—must include random change, which necessitates that quantum nothingness will occasionally become quantum somethingness. Ten to the negative 36 seconds after the singularity, the universe began to inflate faster than the speed of light. Subatomic fluctuations of Heisenberg's uncertainty principle grew from a Planck length to clusters of galaxies hundreds of light-years across in an amount of time too small to measure. The initial inflation stopped at 10 to the negative 33 seconds, and the electromagnetic force binding electrons and atoms popped into existence at 10 to the negative 12 seconds. That allowed for the formation of matter. After that, the universe began to involve energy levels low enough to be reproduced in a particle accelerator, so the rest of creation is known in far greater detail.

"The universe itself could result from less than one milligram of matter compressed to a size billions of times smaller than an electron," writes Linde. "One may consider our part of the universe as an extremely long-lived quantum fluctuation . . . Is it not possible that consciousness, like space-time, has its own intrinsic freedom and that neglecting these will lead to a description of the universe that is fundamentally incomplete?"

One theory holds that consciousness is part of the physical world, like gravity, and participated in the original creation of the universe. A fleeting subatomic particle called the Higgs boson is responsible for the force of gravity and gives matter mass; perhaps a similar unknown particle is responsible for consciousness. It would pervade the universe the way gravity does and, like gravity, determine how everything works. Without it, nothing would exist; the universe would just be a massive wave function. Scientists are so far from explaining consciousness that they can't even agree on a definition, yet it is the crowning achievement of the physical world and seems to be the reason that anything exists in the form that it does. The circularity is audacious: a mix of minerals organized as a human brain summon the world into existence by collapsing its wave function, giving physical reality to the very minerals the brain is made of.

"The mind-body problem is . . . the problem of getting consciousness to arise from biology," writes Donald Hoffman of the Department of Cognitive Sciences at the University of California, Irvine. "So far, no one can build a scientific theory of how this might happen. This failure is so striking that it leads some to wonder if *Homo sapiens* lacks the necessary conceptual apparatus...If you want to solve the mind-body problem, you can take the physical as a given and explain the genesis of the conscious experience, or take conscious experience as a given and explain the genesis of the physical."

But you can't do both.

The word *awe* has been defined as a mix of surprise and fear and is thought to have derived from an archaic English word for *dread*. And it was in exactly that root sense of the word that I began to react to the physics I was reading. I wanted to understand what my father was doing above me in the trauma bay, and eventually I wanted to understand his world and the way he thought. But the closer I got, the more I was filled with a kind of base terror. The secrets that physicists have been prying open made me feel like we were asking for trouble; like we were ungrateful and risking punishment. Is mystery a necessary element of the universe, like gravity, light, and electromagnetic force? Would God be angry if scientists fully explained Him? Could knowing everything result in everything being taken away?

The ultimate transgression of everything that we take to be nature's immutable laws might be something called delayed-choice quantum erasure, and any plausible theory of post-death reality would almost certainly have to involve something this outlandish. It has been well established that observing a double-slit experiment forces photons to act like particles rather than waves and go through one slit at a time, whereas unobserved photons go through both. And it has been well established that particles "entangled" at the quantum level affect each other instantaneously across any distance, including the entire universe. In an attempt to go back in time and erase reality, physicists combined those two phenomena into one experiment that tested entangled particles on the island of La Palma, in the Canaries archipelago, and on the island of Tenerife, eighty-eight miles distant.

(For the brave or merely curious, a slightly abbreviated version of the technical description of this experiment is: "Linearly polarized single photons are sent by a polarization beamsplitter through an interferometer with two spatially separated paths associated with orthogonal S and P polarizations. The movable output beamsplitter consists of the combination of a half-wave plate, a polarization beamsplitter, an electro-optical modulator with its optical axis oriented at 22.5° from input polarizations, and a Wollaston prism. The two beams of the interferometer, which are spatially separated and orthogonally polarized, are first overlapped by the beamsplitter but can still be unambiguously identified by their polarization.")

That is to say, on one island, researchers shot a particle at the double slits, and it passed through both of them as an unobserved wave function. Eighty-eight miles away, via fiber optics cable, they then shot its entangled twin at double slits while observing it with a photon detector; as expected, its wave function collapsed, and it passed through only one slit. But now the universe had a problem: Entangled particles have to do the exact same thing, but the delayed choice had tricked them into acting differently. That was impossible. When researchers checked the strike plate of the first test, though, they found that the wave function *had been retroactively collapsed by the second test and forced through a single slit.* Quantum information had been erased.

The risk of human knowledge not only changes what will happen; it revises what *did* happen and produces a different outcome. In that context, I find myself thinking a lot about the dream I had before I almost died, where I was floating above my family but unable to communicate with them. There was no way to know for sure that it *was* a dream; maybe I *did* die, and that's just what being dead feels like. Dr. Wilson doesn't get the Cordis line into me in time, my coagulants spiral out of control, my heart stops in the trauma bay, and Dr. Kohler dials the phone number I gave him. Barbara answers, and there is that moment of silence when everyone realizes. My daughters look on in confusion, clutched by the babysitters. Uli is on his feet pacing back and forth, "Oh no, oh no." Someone drives Barbara to the hospital to say good-bye to my body and fill out the paperwork. My daughters grow up without a father. My mother goes to her grave after her firstborn. The world goes on. The universe does not notice.

Sometimes I have to grip my head with my hands and tell myself not to start down that path. Sometimes it takes an effort to believe that I didn't die, and that what I'm experiencing now is real. There is a theory that at every moment, all possibilities in our lives are followed, and that an almost infinite multiplicity of universes extends out from each of us eternally. (The one thing the universe has plenty of is space-time, and presumably there would be no problem accommodating such extravagance.) Maybe I died and my family had to go on without me. That makes me want to find them and make sure they are okay. That makes me want to tell them I didn't mean to leave, and that there is a parallel reality—the one I think I'm in right now—where we are all still together.

Another theory of reality is "Leibniz's fearful doctrine of monads," as Schrödinger put it. The theory is impossible to disprove but strangely useless. Gottfried Leibniz was a seventeenth-century mathematician who conceived of a world made up of irreducible particles called monads that, taken to their logical conclusion, meant that each person passes their life alone in a self-referential universe of one. Schrödinger rejected Leibniz by proposing that the universe was constructed in exactly the opposite way: our individual experiences are an illusion that conceals the ultimate reality of one great consciousness. "The mystics of many centuries independently, yet in perfect harmony with each other, have described, each of them, the unique experience of his or her life in terms that can be considered in the phrase, *Deus factum sum*," I have become God.

In such a world, consciousness could never be lost because it's part of the cosmic fabric, and my father as a quantum wave function could welcome me back to the great vastness from which we all come. One might allow the quick thought that it *is* odd that so many religions, so many dying people, so many ecstatics, so many prophets, so many schizophrenics, so many shamans, and so many quantum physicists believe that death is not a final severing but an ultimate merging, and that the reality we take to be life is in fact a passing distraction from something so profound, so real, so all-encompassing, that many return to their paltry bodies on the battlefield or hospital gurney only with great reluctance and a kind of embarrassment. How can I pass up the truth for an illusion? How can I accept this lesser version of myself?

Our universe was created by unknowable forces, has no implicit reason to exist, and seems to violate its own basic laws. In such

a world, what *couldn't* happen? My dead father appearing above me
in a trauma bay is the least of it. When I tried to find the ICU nurse
who had suggested I think about my experience as something sacred rather than something scary, no one at the hospital knew who
she was; no one even knew what I was talking about. It crossed
my mind that she did not exist. My experience was sacred, I finally
decided, because I couldn't really know life until I knew death, and
I couldn't really know death until it came for me. Without death,
life does not require focus or courage or choice. Without death, life
is just an extraordinary stunt that won't stop.

But a universe where consciousness is woven into the very nature of matter would seem to explain both the greatest quantum
puzzles as well as our subjective experience of life. The proposal,
sometimes known as biocentrism, and championed by an American
doctor named Robert Lanza, protects us from an eternity of individual consciousness while still lifting us out of the meaninglessness
of pure biology. Critics say that biocentrism is not a legitimate theory because it can't be tested, but that doesn't mean it's wrong. If
consciousness comprises an essential part of the physical universe,
the very idea of testing its existence may be a logical impossibility.

The word *apocalypse* comes from the Greek, *apokalupsis*, to
"uncover," because all knowledge is said to be revealed in the final
collapse. A last, terrifying, theory proposes that it is cosmically pro-
hibited to have that knowledge beforehand because consciousness
cannot survive a complete understanding of itself, and as physicists
get closer to the final, apocalyptic truth, test results become more
and more unreliable until, for example, entangled particles in Tenerife appear to reach back and fix outcomes for twinned particles in

La Palma, and our credulity around such things is how the cosmos reaches back to trick *us* and fix a far greater outcome: that the ultimate truth must never be known, because once the knower understands that he is the entirety of all things, the universe becomes fatally self-referential and collapses back into a closed spacetime of zero radius with all values headed to zero and all history annihilated.

When I was sixteen or seventeen, I convinced my father to go camping with me in the White Mountains of New Hampshire. He had never slept outside, and I thought it was time. It was late October, and dark came on faster than we expected and with it, the cold. We found ourselves in a forest of dwarf spruce just below the tree line looking for a place to sleep. It was then that I noticed that my father wasn't making much sense. He was strangely passive, like a child, and disinterested in what was happening around him. We were miles into the woods and completely alone; I was going to have to figure this out.

I put the tent up and unrolled a sleeping bag and told my father to get in. He was shaking badly and almost certainly had hypothermia. There was just enough light to gather firewood, and I got a flame going in some birch bark and fed it until there was a little circle of warmth in the great boreal darkness around us. I crouched at its edge stirring a pot of soup and then poured the soup into tin cups and brought them in to my father. He waved his away, mumbling that he just wanted to go to sleep, but I insisted, and he finally took a sip. We sat cross-legged, drinking soup and talking about our plans for the morning. As my father warmed up, he returned to being my father, and I returned to being his son.

After a while he said he was tired, and he lay back and closed his eyes. I sat there watching his chest rise and fall until I was sure he was asleep. I'm now much older than he was that night, and I finally understand how much my father must have trusted me on that trip, how much he must have loved me. We're all on the side of a mountain shocked by how fast it's gotten dark; the only question is whether we're with people we love or not. There is no other thing—no belief or religion or faith—there is just that. Just the knowledge that when we finally close our eyes, someone will be there to watch over us as we head out into that great, soaring night.

# *Author's Note on Blood Donation*

I survived a ruptured aneurysm in my pancreatic artery in part because I received ten units of blood to replace what I'd lost into my abdomen. In other words, ten anonymous blood donors helped save my life. In gratitude, I now donate blood as often as I'm allowed—roughly three or four times a year. Please donate blood at your nearest blood bank; you may well save the life of a child or a parent, and one day you may need blood yourself. Donating blood is painless, safe, and takes less than an hour. There aren't many ways to be part of something greater than yourself, and donating blood is one of the easiest and finest. You can find the blood donation center nearest to you at: www.donatingblood.org.

# Acknowledgments

First and foremost, I must thank the incredible staff at Cape Cod Hospital in Hyannis for saving my life—particularly doctors Steve Kohler, Spencer Wilson, Craig Cornwall, Phil Dombrowski, and Daniel Gorin. Additionally, Joe Lang—who was in the ambulance with me—and his wife, Sara, agreed to talk to me about my experience, as did several of the doctors who treated me. Interventional radiologists Dr. Lynn Brody and Dr. Richard Baum, and former combat medic Dr. Eric Goralnick, agreed to interviews and helped me understand this incredibly complex topic. I must also thank Dr. Christian Koch, Rachel Rackow, Deirdre Barrett, Dr. Jeff Rediger, Dr. Justin Sanders, Dr. Sarah Abedi, and Kelly Paterson for talking to me at length and helping guide my research. I am also enormously grateful to a young medical student named Charlotte, who provided comfort to my wife at an exceedingly difficult moment.

Much of the research was generated by Ami Karlage, to whom I am enormously indebted. Additionally, my friend Arin Hirst gave me crucial guidance on some of the more abstract principles of subatomic physics and entropy. Christian Rogowski, to whom I was introduced by my friend Alex Bruskin, went to great lengths to translate a poem Erwin Schrödinger wrote longhand for my great-aunt Ithi. (The poem does not appear in the book, but I am enormously grateful to have the translation; Schrödinger was a far better physicist than poet.) My father's colleagues, Joel Garrelick and Rudolph Martinez, indulged my endless questions about physics and read my manuscript for factual errors. All the interviews I did were transcribed with incredible accuracy by Kathryn Drury. I must also thank my agent, Stuart Krichevsky, and his assistant, Aemilia Phillips, as well as editors Sean Manning and Jonathan Karp at Simon & Schuster, along with Julia Prosser, Cat Boyd, Jonathan Evans, and Stephen Bedford. Rob Leaver read and reread the manuscript and helped enormously in the final stages of the writing. Teo, who attended to both my mother and father as they died, did something so profound and important for my family that it's hard to know how to properly thank her.

Finally, I must thank Barbara for reading many drafts of the manuscript, providing crucial insights, asking great questions, and insisting that the ambulance crew take me to the hospital.

# Sources

First and foremost, my basic understanding of the medical danger I was in—and how it was resolved—came from interviews with Dr. Steve Kohler and Dr. Craig Cornwall, of Cape Cod Hospital, in Hyannis. Dr. Eric Goralnick of Brigham and Women's Hospital, in Boston, also provided crucial insight into my case and the amazing technology around it. A wonderful book called *Who Goes First*, by Dr. Lawrence Altman, provided almost the entirety of the information on how the venous catheter was invented.

There is a huge body of literature devoted to near-death experiences, but the most prominent and useful books for my research were: *What Happens When We Die* and *Erasing Death*, by Dr. Sam Parnia; *After*, by Dr. Bruce Greyson; *Experiences Near Death* and *A Social History of Dying*, by Allan Kellehear; *The Science of Near-Death Experiences*, by John C. Hagan III (editor); *Deathbed Visions*, by Sir William Barrett; *The Worm at the Core*, by Sheldon Solomon, Jeffrey Greenberg, and Tom Pyszczynski; and *The Spiritual Doorway in the Brain*, by Dr. Kevin Nelson. The related topic of life, death, and science was taken from two amazing books: *What Is Life?*, by Addy Pross; and *Every Life Is on Fire*, by Jeremy England.

The definitive biography of Erwin Schrödinger is *Schrödinger: Life and Thought* by Walter Moore. The book confirms my family's stories of his affair with my great-aunt Ithi; in fact, my father reviewed the book for a scientific publication. Schrödinger's popular books, *My View of the World* and *What Is Life?*, also provide great insight into the mind of this extraordinary man. There are scores of books on subatomic physics, consciousness, and cosmology, but the ones I relied on are: *Thirty Years That Shook Physics*, by George Gamow; *Quantum Enigma*, by Bruce Rosenblum and Fred Kuttner; *Biocentrism*, by Dr. Robert Lanza with Bob Berman; *Mindful Universe*, by Henry P. Stapp; *Quantum Questions*, by Ken Wilber (editor); *Why Does the World Exist*, by Jim Holt; and *Consciousness*, by Susan Blackmore.

Additionally, I referred to the following research papers, here organized by category. Not all of this material found its way into my book, but taken as a whole, it formed the huge body of knowledge that informed my work.

Finally, it must be noted that a small number of names were changed to protect the privacy of certain individuals.

## MEDICAL RESEARCH

Agar, M., Y. Alici, and W. S. Breitbart. "Delirium." In *Oxford Textbook of Palliative Medicine*, edited by N. Cherny et al., 1092–1100. Oxford: Oxford University Press, 2015.

Armstrong, M. B., K. S. Stadtlander, and M. K. Grove. "Pancreaticoduodenal Artery Aneurysm Associated with Median Arcuate Ligament Syndrome." *Annals of Vascular Surgery* 28, no. 3 (2014): 741.e1–741.e5.

Babic, A. M., and C. D. Hillyer. "Overview of Adverse Events and Outcomes Following Transfusion." In *Transfusion Medicine and Hemostasis: Clinical and Laboratory Aspects*, edited by B. H. Shaz, C. D. Hillyer, M. Roshal, and C. S. Abrams, 383–387. Amsterdam: Elsevier, 2013.

Black, S. "Our Cells and Ourselves." In *All That Remains: A Renowned Forensic Scientist on Death, Mortality, and Solving Crimes*, 31–60. New York: Arcade Publishing, 2018.

Chan, R. P., and E. David. "Reperfusion of Splanchnic Artery Aneurysm Following Transcatheter Embolization: Treatment with Percutaneous Thrombin Injection." *CardioVascular and Interventional Radiology* 27, no. 3 (2004): 264–267.

Chiang, K. S., C. M. Johnson, M. A. McKusick, T. P. Maus, and A. W. Stanson. "Management of Inferior Pancreaticoduodenal Artery Aneurysms: A 4-Year, Single Center Experience." *CardioVascular and Interventional Radiology* 17, no. 4 (1994): 217–221.

Cope, C., and R. Zeit. "Coagulation of Aneurysms by Direct Percutaneous Thrombin Injection." *American Journal of Roentgenology* 147, no. 2 (1986): 383–387.

De Perrot, M., T. Berney, J. Deleaval, L. Buhler, G. Mentha, and P. Morel. "Management of True Aneurysms of the Pancreaticoduodenal Arteries." *Annals of Surgery* 229, no. 3 (1999): 416–420.

Devery, K., D. Rawlings, J. Tieman, and R. Damarel. "Deathbed Phenomena Reported by Patients in Palliative Care: Clinical Opportunities and Responses." *International Journal of Palliative Nursing* 21, no. 3 (2015): 24–32.

Ferguson, F. "Aneurysm of the Superior Pancreaticoduodenalis, with Perforation into the Common Bile Duct." *Proceedings of the New York Pathological Society* 24 (1895).

Flood, K., and A. A. Nicholson. "Inferior Pancreaticoduodenal Artery Aneurysms Associated with Occlusive Lesions of the Celiac Axis: Diagnosis, Treatment Options, Outcomes, and Review of the Literature." *CardioVascular and Interventional Radiology* 36, no. 3 (2013): 578–587.

Ghassemi, A., D. Javit, and E. H. Dillon. "Thrombin Injection of a Pancreaticoduodenal Artery Pseudoaneurysm After Failed Attempts at Transcatheter Embolization." *Journal of Vascular Surgery* 43, no. 3 (2006): 618–622.

Goodnough, L. T., M. E. Brecher, M. H. Kanter, and J. P. AuBuchon. "Transfusion Medicine. First of Two Parts—Blood Transfusion." *New England Journal of Medicine* 340, no. 6 (1999): 438–447.

Hagisawa, K., M. Kinoshita, H. Sakai, and S. Takeoka. "Artificial Blood Transfusion: A New Chapter in an Old Story." *Physiology News* (March 2021).

Heidrich, D. E., and N. K. English. "Delirium." In *Care of the Imminently Dying*, edited by B. Farrell et al., 1–22. Oxford: Oxford University Press, 2015.

Hillyer, C. D. "Blood Banking and Transfusion Medicine—History, Industry, and Discipline." In *Transfusion Medicine and Hemostasis: Clinical and Laboratory Aspects*, edited by B. H. Shaz, C. D. Hillyer, M. Roshal, and C. S. Abrams, 3–9. Amsterdam: Elsevier, 2013.

Hooper, N., and T. J. Armstrong. "Hemorrhagic Shock." *StatPearls*. Treasure Island, FL: StatPearls Publishing, 2021.

Horiguchi, A., S. Ishihara, M. Ito et al. "Multislice CT Study of Pancreatic Head Arterial Dominance." *Journal of Hepato-Biliary-Pancreatic Surgery* 15, no. 3 (2008): 322–326.

Hospice Foundation website, "Signs of Approaching Death," https://

hospicefoundation.org/Hospice-Care/Signs-of-Approaching -Death.

Ikeda, O., Y. Tamura, Y. Nakasone, K. Kawanaka, and Y. Yamashita. "Coil Embolization of Pancreaticoduodenal Artery Aneurysms Associated with Celiac Artery Stenosis: Report of Three Cases." *CardioVascular and Interventional Radiology* 30, no. 3 (May–June 2007): 504–507.

Ikoma, A. "Inferior Pancreaticoduodenal Artery Aneurysm Treated with Coil Packing and Stent Placement." *World Journal of Radiology* 4, no. 8 (2012): 387.

Izumi, M., M. Ryu, A. Cho et al. "Ruptured Pancreaticoduodenal Artery Aneurysm Treated by Superselective Transcatheter Arterial Embolization and Preserving Vascularity of Pancreaticoduodenal Arcades." *Journal of Hepato-Biliary-Pancreatic Surgery* 11, no. 2 (2004): 145–148.

Jimenez J. C., F. Rafidi, and L. Morris. "True Celiac Artery Aneurysm Secondary to Median Arcuate Ligament Syndrome." *Vascular and Endovascular Surgery* 45, no. 3 (2011): 288–289.

Jimenez, J. C., M. Harlander-Locke, and E. P. Dutson. "Open and Laparoscopic Treatment of Median Arcuate Ligament Syndrome." *Journal of Vascular Surgery* 56, no. 3 (2012): 869–873.

Katsura, M., M. Gushimiyagi, H. Takara, and H. Mototake. "True Aneurysm of the Pancreaticoduodenal Arteries: A Single Institution Experience." *Journal of Gastrointestinal Surgery* 14, no. 9 (2010): 1409–1413.

Koganemaru, M., T. Abe, M. Nonoshita et al. "Follow-up of True Visceral Artery Aneurysm After Coil Embolization by Three-Dimensional Contrast-Enhanced MR Angiography." *Diagnostic and Interventional Radiology* 20, no. 2 (2014): 129–135.

Lacey, J. "Management of the Actively Dying Patient." In *Oxford*

*Textbook of Palliative Medicine*, edited by N. Cherny et al., 1125–1133. Oxford: Oxford University Press, 2015.

Lasheras, J. C. "The Biomechanics of Arterial Aneurysms." In *Annual Review of Fluid Mechanics* 39, no. 1 (January 2007): 293–319.

Lossing, A. G., H. Grosman, R. A. Mustard, and E. M. Hatswell. "Emergency Embolization of a Ruptured Aneurysm of the Pancreaticoduodenal Arcade." *Canadian Journal of Surgery* 38, no. 4 (1995): 363–365.

Loukas, M., J. Pinyard, S. Vaid, C. Kinsella, A. Tariq, and R. S. Tubbs. "Clinical Anatomy of Celiac Artery Compression Syndrome: A Review." *Clinical Anatomy* 20, no. 6 (2007): 612–617.

Lowey, Susan E. *Nursing Care at the End of Life: What Every Clinician Should Know*. Open SUNY. New York: Milne, 2015.

Mano, Y., Y. Takehara, T. Sakaguchi et al. "Hemodynamic Assessment of Celiaco-Mesenteric Anastomosis in Patients with Pancreaticoduodenal Artery Aneurysm Concomitant with Celiac Artery Occlusion Using Flow-Sensitive Four-Dimensional Magnetic Resonance Imaging." *European Journal of Vascular and Endovascular Surgery* 46, no. 3 (2013): 321–328.

National Institutes of Health, National Institute on Aging. "Providing Care and Comfort at the End of Life," https://www.nia.nih.gov/health/providing-comfort-end-life.

Norfolk, D. *Handbook of Transfusion Medicine*, 5th ed. Norwich, UK: TSO, 2013.

Nosher, J. L., J. Chung, L. S. Brevetti, A. M. Graham, and R. L. Siegel. "Visceral and Renal Artery Aneurysms: A Pictorial Essay on Endovascular Therapy." *Radiographics* 26, no. 6 (2006) 1687–1704.

"Palliative and End-of-Life Care." In *Harrison's Manual of Medicine*, 20th ed., edited by J. Larry Jameson et al. New York: McGraw

Hill, 2020, https://accessmedicine.mhmedical.com/content .aspx?bookid=2738&sectionid=227555538.

Pang, T. C. Y., R. Maher, S. Gananadha, T. J. Hugh, and J. S. Samra. "Peripancreatic Pseudoaneurysms: A Management-Based Classification System." *Surgical Endoscopy and Other Interventional Techniques* 28, no. 7 (2014): 2027–2038.

Rossi, E. C., and T. L. Simon. "Transfusion in the New Millennium." In *Rossi's Principles of Transfusion Medicine*, 4th ed., edited by T. L. Simon, E. L. Snyder, B. G. Solheim et al., 1–14. Hoboken, NJ: Blackwell Publishing, 2009.

Sachdev-Ost, U. "Visceral Artery Aneurysms: Review of Current Management Options." *Mount Sinai Journal of Medicine* 77, no. 3 (2010): 296–303.

Savastano, S., G. P. Feltrin, D. Miotto, M. Chiesura-Corona, and P. Sandri. "Embolization of Ruptured Aneurysm of the Pancreaticoduodenal Artery Secondary to Long-Standing Stenosis of the Celiac Axis: Case Reports." *Vascular and Endovascular Surgery* 29, no. 4 (1995): 309–314.

Scovell, S., and A. Hamdan. "Celiac Artery Compression Syndrome." UpToDate.com, January 28, 2021, accessed August 17, 2021.

Sgroi, M. D., N. Kabutey, M. Krishnam, and R. M. Fujitani. "Pancreaticoduodenal Artery Aneurysms Secondary to Median Arcuate Ligament Syndrome May Not Need Celiac Artery Revascularization or Ligament Release." *Annals of Vascular Surgery* 29, no. 1 (2015): 122.e1–122.e7.

Shaz, B. H., and C. D. Hillyer. "Massive Transfusion." In *Transfusion Medicine and Hemostasis: Clinical and Laboratory Aspects,* edited by B. H. Shaz, C. D. Hillyer, M. Roshal, and C. S. Abrams, 367–372. Amsterdam: Elsevier, 2013.

Shi, P. A. "Patient Blood Management." In *Transfusion Medicine and*

*Hemostasis: Clinical and Laboratory Aspects*, edited by B. H. Shaz, C. D. Hillyer, M. Roshal, and C. S. Abrams, 373–381. Amsterdam: Elsevier, 2013.

Stambo, G. W., M. J. Hallisey, and J. J. Gallagher. "Arteriographic Embolization of Visceral Artery Pseudoaneurysms." *Annals of Vascular Surgery* 10, no. 5 (1996): 476–480.

Stanford Palliative Care Center of Excellence website, https://palliative.stanford.edu/transition-to-death/signs-of-impending-death/.

Sumpio, B. "Overview of Visceral Artery Aneurysm and Pseudoaneurysm." UpToDate.com, November 24, 2020, accessed August 17, 2021.

——. "Treatment of Visceral Artery Aneurysm and Pseudoaneurysm." UpToDate.com, November 24, 2020, accessed August 17, 2021.

Sutton, D., and G. Lawton. "Coeliac Stenosis or Occlusion with Aneurysm of the Collateral Supply." *Clinical Radiology* 24, no. 1 (January 1973): 49–53.

Suzuki, K., H. Kashimura, M. Sato et al. "Pancreaticoduodenal Artery Aneurysms Associated with Celiac Axis Stenosis Due to Compression by Median Arcuate Ligament and Celiac Plexus." *Journal of Gastroenterology* 33, no. 3 (June 1998): 434–438.

Suzuki, K., Y. Tachi, S. Ito et al. "Endovascular Management of Ruptured Pancreaticoduodenal Artery Aneurysms Associated with Celiac Axis Stenosis." *CardioVascular and Interventional Radiology* 31, no. 6 (2008): 1082–1087.

Takao, H., I. Doi, T. Watanabe, N. Yoshioka, and K. Ohtomo. "Natural History of True Pancreaticoduodenal Artery Aneurysms."

*British Journal of Radiology* 83, no. 993 (September 2010): 744–746.

Tarazov, P. G., A. M. Ignashov, A. V. Pavlovskij, and A. S. Novikova. "Pancreaticoduodenal Artery Aneurysm Associated with Celiac Axis Stenosis: Combined Angiographic and Surgical Treatment." *Digestive Diseases and Sciences* 46, no. 6 (June 2001): 1232–1235.

Tien, Y.-W., H.-L. Kao, and H.-P. Wang. "Celiac Artery Stenting: A New Strategy for Patients with Pancreaticoduodenal Artery Aneurysm Associated with Stenosis of the Celiac Artery." *Journal of Gastroenterology* 39, no. 1 (2004): 81–85.

Tisdale, S. "A Good Death." In *Advice for Future Corpses (and Those Who Love Them): A Practical Perspective on Death and Dying*. New York: Gallery Books, 2018, 39–62.

Tori, M., M. Nakahara, H. Akamatsu, S. Ueshima, M. Shimizu, and K. Nakao. "Significance of Intraoperative Monitoring of Arterial Blood Flow Velocity and Hepatic Venous Oxygen Saturation for Performing Minimally Invasive Surgery in a Patient with Multiple Calcified Pancreaticoduodenal Aneurysms with Celiac Artery Occlusion." *Journal of Hepato-Biliary-Pancreatic Surgery* 13, no. 5 (2006): 472–476.

Upchurch, G. R., G. B. Zelenock, and J. C. Stanley. "Splanchnic Artery Aneurysms." In *Vascular Surgery*, 6th ed., edited by R. B. Rutherford, 1565–1581. Philadelphia: W. B. Saunders, 2005.

## NEAR-DEATH EXPERIENCES

Aminoff, M. J., M. M. Scheinman, J. C. Griffin, and J. M. Herre. "Electrocerebral Accompaniments of Syncope Associated with

Malignant Ventricular Arrhythmias." *Annals of Internal Medicine* 108 (1988): 791–796.

Aspect, A., et al. "Experimental Tests of Realistic Local Theories via Bell's Theorem." *Physical Review Letters* 47, no. 7 (1981): 460–463.

Bailey, L. W. "A 'Little Death': The Near-Death Experience and Tibetan *Delogs.*" *Journal of Near-Death Studies* 19, no. 3 (Spring 2001): 139–159.

Black, D. W., and J. E. Grant, eds. *DSM-5 Guidebook: The Essential Companion to the Diagnostic and Statistical Manual of Mental Disorders*, 5th ed. Washington, DC: American Psychiatric Publishing, 2014.

Blackmore, S. "Near-Death Experiences." In *The Skeptic Encyclopedia of Pseudoscience*, edited by M. Shermer, 152–157. Santa Barbara, CA: ABC-CLIO, 2002.

Blanke, O., and S. Dieguez. "Leaving Body and Life Behind: Out-of-Body and Near-Death Experience." In *The Neurology of Consciousness*, edited by S. Laureys and G. Tononi, 303–325. Amsterdam: Elsevier, 2009.

Blanke, O., N. Faivre, and S. Dieguez. "Leaving Body and Life Behind: Out-of-Body and Near-Death Experience." In *The Neurology of Consciousness*, 2nd ed., edited by S. Laureys, O. Gosseries, and G. Tononi, 323–347. Amsterdam: Elsevier, 2016.

Braude, S. E. *First Person Plural: Multiple Personality and the Philosophy of Mind.* New York: Routledge, 1991.

Carhart-Harris, R. L., et al. "Neural Correlates of the Psychedelic State as Determined by fMRI Studies with Psilocybin." *Proceedings of the National Academy of Sciences of the United States of America* 109, no. 6 (2012): 2138–2143.

Carhart-Harris, R. L., et al. "Neural Correlates of the LSD Experience

Revealed by Multimodal Neuroimaging." *Proceedings of the National Academy of Sciences of the United States of America* (PNAS Early Edition) 113, no. 17 (April 2016), https://doi .org/10.1073/pnas.1518377113.

Carr, D. B., and M. Prendergast. "Endorphins at the Approach of Death." *Lancet* 317, no. 8216 (1981): 343–400.

Carr, D. B. "Pathophysiology of Stress-Induced Limbic Lobe Dysfunction: A Hypothesis for NDEs." *Anabiosis—The Journal for Near-Death Studies* 2 (1982): 75–89.

Cassol, Helena, et al. "Memories of Near-Death Experiences: Are They Self-Defining?" *Neuroscience of Consciousness* 2019, no. 1, niz002 (2019), https://doi.org/10.1093/nc/niz002.

Conn, Henry R. "The Mental Universe." *Nature* 436 (July 6, 2005): 29.

Cook, E. W., B. Greyson, and I. Stevenson. "Do Any Near-Death Experiences Provide Evidence for the Survival of Human Personality After Death? Relevant Features and Illustrative Case Reports." *Journal of Scientific Exploration* 12, no. 3 (1998): 377–406.

Craffert, P. F. "Making Sense of Near-Death Experience Research: Circumstance Specific Alterations of Consciousness." *Anthropology of Consciousness* 30, no. 1 (2019): 64–89.

DeVries, J. W., P. F. Bakker, G. H. Visser, J. C. Diephuis, and A. C. van Huffelen. "Changes in Cerebral Oxygen Uptake and Cerebral Electrical Activity During Defibrillation Threshold Testing." *Anesthesiology and Analgesia* 87, no. 1 (1998): 16–20.

Eagleman, D. *Incognito: The Secret Lives of the Brain.* New York: Canongate, 2011.

Fracasso, C., S. Aleyasin, H. Friedman, and M. Young. "Near-Death Experiences Among a Sample of Iranian Muslims." *Journal of Near-Death Studies* 29 (2010): 271.

French, C. C. "Near-Death Experiences in Cardiac Arrest Survivors." *Progress in Brain Research* 150 (2005): 351–367.

Friston, K., B. Sengupta, and G. Auletta. "Cognitive Dynamics: From Attractors to Active Inference." *Proceedings of the IEEE* 102, no. 4 (2014): 427–445.

Green, J. T. "Near-Death Experiences, Shamanism, and the Scientific Method." *Journal of Near-Death Studies* 16, no. 3 (1998): 205–222.

———. "The Near-Death Experience as a Shamanic Initiation: A Case Study." *Journal of Near-Death Studies* 19, no. 4 (2001): 209–225.

Greyson, B., E. W. Kelly, and E. F. Kelly. "Explanatory Models for Near-Death Experiences." In *The Handbook of Near-Death Experiences: Thirty Years of Investigation*, edited by J. M. Holden, B. Greyson, and D. James, 226. Santa Barbara, CA: Praeger/ABC-CLIO, 2009.

Greyson, B. "Incidence and Correlates of Near-Death Experiences in a Cardiac Care Unit." *General Hospital Psychiatry* 25 (2003): 269–276.

———. "The Near-Death Experience Scale: Construction, Reliability and Validity." *Journal of Nervous and Mental Disease* 171 (2003): 369–375.

———. "Seeing Deceased Persons Not Known to Have Died: 'Peak in Darien' Experiences." *Anthropology & Humanism* 35 (2010): 159–171.

Griffiths, R. R., et al. "Psilocybin Can Occasion Mystical-Type Experiences Having Substantial and Sustained Personal Meaning and Spiritual Significance." *Psychopharmacology* 187 (2006): 268–283.

Gröblacher, S., et al. "An Experimental Test of Non-Local Realism." *Nature* 446 (2007): 871–875.

Guerra-Doce, E., et al. "Direct Evidence of the Use of Multiple

Drugs in Bronze Age Menorca (Western Mediterranean) from Human Hair Analysis." *Nature* 13, no. 4782 (2023).

Heflick, N. A., et al. "Death Awareness and Body–Self Dualism: A Why and How of Afterlife Belief." *European Journal of Social Psychology* 45, no. 2 (2015): 267–275.

Holden, J. M., J. Long, and B. J. MacLurg. "Characteristics of Western Near-Death Experiencers." In *The Handbook of Near-Death Experiences: Thirty Years of Investigation*, edited by J. Holden, B. Greyson, and D. James, 109–134. Santa Barbara, CA: ABC-CLIO, 2009.

Holden, J. M. "Veridical Perception in Near-Death Experiences." In *The Handbook of Near-Death Experiences: Thirty Years of Investigation*, edited by J. Holden, B. Greyson, and D. James, 185–211. Santa Barbara, CA: ABC-CLIO, 2009.

John, E., et al. "Invariant Reversible QEEG Effects of Anesthetics." *Consciousness & Cognition* 10 (2001): 165–183.

Judson, I. R., and E. Wiltshaw. "A Near-Death Experience." *Lancet* 2, no. 8349 (1983): 561–562.

Kellehear, A. "Census of Non-Western Near-Death Experiences to 2005: Observations and Critical Reflections." In *The Handbook of Near-Death Experiences: Thirty Years of Investigation*, edited by J. Holden, B. Greyson, and D. James, 135–158. Santa Barbara, CA: ABC-CLIO, 2009.

———. *Visitors at the End of Life: Finding Meaning and Purpose in Near-Death Phenomena*. New York: Columbia University Press, 2019.

Kelly, E. F., et al. *Irreducible Mind: Toward a Psychology for the 21st Century*. Lanham, MD: Rowman & Littlefield, 2009.

Kelly, E. W., B. Greyson, and I. Stevenson. "Can Experiences Near Death Furnish Evidence of Life After Death?" *Omega* 40, no. 4 (1999–2000): 513–519.

Kelly, E. W. "Near-Death Experiences with Reports of Meeting Deceased People." *Death Studies* 25 (2001): 229–249.

Kim, Y.-H., et al. "A Delayed 'Choice' Quantum Eraser." *Physical Review Letters* 84 (2000): 1–5.

Koch, C. *The Quest for Consciousness: A Neurobiological Approach.* Englewood, CO: Roberts & Company, 2004.

———. "What Near-Death Experiences Reveal about the Brain." *Scientific American*, June 1, 2020.

Lake, James. "The Near-Death Experience (NDE) as an Inherited Predisposition: Possible Genetic, Epigenetic, Neural and Symbolic Mechanisms." *Medical Hypotheses* 126 (2019): 135–148.

Lapkiewicz, R., et al. "Experimental Non-Classicality of an Indivisible Quantum System." *Nature* 474 (2011): 490–493.

Leggett, A. N. "Nonlocal Hidden-Variable Theories and Quantum Mechanics: An Incompatibility Theorem." *Foundations of Physics* 33, no. 10 (2003): 1469–1493.

Liester, M. B. "Near-Death Experiences and Ayahuasca-Induced Experiences—Two Unique Pathways to a Phenomenologically Similar State of Consciousness." *Journal of Transpersonal Psychology* 45, no. 1 (2013): 24–48.

Linde, A. "Universe, Life, Consciousness." A paper delivered at the Physics and Cosmology Group of the Science and Spiritual Quest program of the Center for Theology and the Natural Sciences (CTNS), Berkeley, California (1998), accessed June 14, 2016, https://web.stanford.edu/~alinde/SpirQuest.doc.

Long, J., with P. Perry. *Evidence of the Afterlife: The Science of Near-Death Experiences.* New York: HarperCollins, 2010.

Lynch, J. R., and C. Kilmartin. *Overcoming Masculine Depression: The Pain Behind the Mask.* New York: Routledge, 2013.

Martial, C., et al. "Neurochemical Models of Near-Death Experiences: A Large-Scale Study Based on the Semantic Similarity of Written Reports." *Consciousness and Cognition* 69 (2019): 52–69.

Merali, Z. "Quantum 'Spookiness' Passes Toughest Test Yet." *Nature*, August 27, 2015, accessed August 30, 2015, http://www.nature .com/news/quantum-spookiness-passes-toughest-test-yet-1 .18255.

Mobbs, D., and C. Watt. "There Is Nothing Paranormal About Near-Death Experiences: How Neuroscience Can Explain Seeing Bright Lights, Meeting the Dead, or Being Convinced You Are One of Them." *Trends in Cognitive Sciences* 15, no. 10 (2011): 447–449.

Moody, R. A. *Life After Life*. Covington, GA: Mockingbird Books, 1975.

Moorjani, A. *Dying to Be Me: My Journey from Cancer, to Near Death, to True Healing*. Carlsbad, CA: Hay House, 2012.

Morse, M. L., D. Venicia, and J. Milstein. "Near-Death Experiences: A Neurophysiologic Explanatory Model." *Journal of Near-Death Studies* 8, no. 1 (1989): 45–53.

Nahm, M., and J. Nicolay. "Essential Features of Eight Published Muslim Near-Death Experiences: An Addendum to Joel Ibrahim Kreps's 'The Search for Muslim Near-Death Experiences.'" *Journal of Near-Death Studies* 29, no. 1 (2010): 255–263.

Osis, K., and E. Haraldsson. *At the Hour of Death*. 3rd ed. New York: Avon, 1977.

Palhano-Fontes, F., et al. "The Psychedelic State Induced by Ayahuasca Modulates the Activity and Connectivity of the Default Mode Network." *PLoS ONE* 10, no. 2 (2015).

Parnia, S., and P. Fenwick. "Near Death Experiences in Cardiac Arrest: Visions of a Dying Brain or Visions of a New Science of Consciousness." *Resuscitation* 52, no. 1 (2002): 5–11.

Parnia, S., D. G. Waller, R. Yeates, and P. Fenwick. "A Qualitative and Quantitative Study of the Incidence, Features and Aetiology of Near Death Experiences in Cardiac Arrest Survivors." *Resuscitation* 48, no. 2 (2001):149–156,

Peinkhofer, C., J. P. Dreier, and D. Kondziella. "Semiology and Mechanisms of Near-Death Experiences." *Current Neurology and Neuroscience Reports* 19 (2019): 1–12.

Peinkhofer, C., et al. "The Evolutionary Origin of Near-Death Experiences: A Systematic Investigation." *Brain Communications* 3, no. 3 (2021): fcab132.

Ring, K., and S. Cooper. *Mindsight: Near-Death and Out-of-Body Experiences in the Blind.* Palo Alto, CA: William James Center for Consciousness Studies, Institute of Transpersonal Psychology, 1999.

Ring, K., and E. E. Valarino. "Introduction." In *Lessons from the Light: What We Can Learn from the Near-Death Experience*, 1–10. Needham, NH: Moment Point Press, 2006.

———. "Living in the Light: Afterward." In *Lessons from the Light: What We Can Learn from the Near-Death Experience*, 123–144. Needham, NH: Moment Point Press, 2006.

Robinson, H. "Dualism." In *The Stanford Encyclopedia of Philosophy*, edited by E. N. Zalta. Spring 2016, accessed June 17, 2016, http://plato.stanford.edu/archives/spr2016/entries/dualism.

Saavedra-Aguilar, J. C., and J. S. Gómez-Jeria. "A Neurobiological Model for Near-Death Experiences." *Journal of Near-Death Studies* 7, no. 4 (1989): 205–222.

Sabom, M. *Recollections of Death: A Medical Investigation.* New York: Simon & Schuster, 1982.

Sartori, P. *The Near-Death Experiences of Hospitalized Intensive Care*

*Patients: A Five-Year Clinical Study.* Lewiston, NY: Edwin Mellen Press, 2008.

Schlumpf, Y. R., et al. "Dissociative Part-Dependent Resting-State Activity in Dissociative Identity Disorder: A Controlled fMRI Perfusion Study." *PLoS ONE* 9, no. 6 (2014).

Schwaninger, J., P. R. Eisenberg, K. B. Schechtman, and A. N. Weiss. "A Prospective Analysis of Near-Death Experiences in Cardiac Arrest Patients." *Journal of Near-Death Studies* 20 (2002): 215–232.

Stoljar, D. "Physicalism." In *The Stanford Encyclopedia of Philosophy,* edited by E. N. Zalta. Spring 2016, accessed June 14, 2016, http://plato.stanford.edu/archives/spr2016/entries/physicalism/.

Strasburger, H., and B. Waldvogel. "Sight and Blindness in the Same Person: Gating in the Visual System." *PsyCh Journal* 4, no. 4 (2015): 178–185.

Strassman, R. *DMT: The Spirit Molecule.* Rochester, VT: Park Street Press, 2001.

Strassman, R., et al. *Inner Paths to Outer Space.* Rochester, VT: Park Street Press, 2008.

Sutherland, C. "Trailing Clouds of Glory: The Near-Death Experiences of Western Children and Teens." In *The Handbook of Near-Death Experiences: Thirty Years of Investigation,* edited by J. Holden, B. Greyson, and D. James, 93. Santa Barbara, CA: ABC-CLIO, 2009.

Timmermann, C., et al. "DMT Models the Near-Death Experience." *Frontiers in Psychology* 9 (2018): article 1424.

van Lommel, P., R. van Wees, V. Meyers, and I. Elfferich. "Near-Death Experience in Survivors of Cardiac Arrest: A Prospective Study in the Netherlands." *Lancet* 358 (2001): 2039–2045.

Vicente, P., et al. "Enhanced Interplay of Neuronal Coherence and Coupling in the Dying Human Brain." *Frontiers in Aging Neuroscience* 14, no. 8. February 22, 2022, https://doi.org/10.3389/fnagi.2022.813531.

Whinnery, J. E. "Psychophysiologic Correlates of Unconsciousness and Near-Death Experiences." *Journal of Near-Death Studies* 15, no. 4 (1997): 231–258.

White, N. S., and M. T. Alkire. "Impaired Thalamocortical Connectivity in Humans During General-Anesthetic-Induced Unconsciousness." *NeuroImage* 19 (2003): 402–411.

Zingrone, N. L., and C. S. Alvarado. "Pleasurable Western Adult Near-Death Experiences: Features, Circumstances, and Incidence." In *The Handbook of Near-Death Experiences: Thirty Years of Investigation*, edited by J. Holden, B. Greyson, and D. James, 17–40. Santa Barbara, CA: ABC-CLIO, 2009.

## SUBATOMIC PHYSICS, COSMOLOGY, AND CONSCIOUSNESS

Ananthaswamy, A. "Quantum Magic Trick Shows Reality Is What You Make It." *New Scientist*, June 22, 2011, https://www.newscientist.com/article/dn20600-quantum-magic-trick-shows-reality-is-what-you-make-it/.

Bell, J. "On the Einstein Podolsky Rosen Paradox." *Physics* 1, no. 3 (1964): 195–200.

Cartwright, J. "Quantum Physics Says Goodbye to Reality." *Physics World*, April 20, 2007, http://physicsworld.com/a/quantum-physics-says-goodbye-to-reality.

Chalmers, D. "Consciousness and Its Place in Nature." In *The*

*Blackwell Guide to the Philosophy of Mind*, edited by S. Stich and F. Warfield. Malden, MA: Blackwell Publishing, 2003.

Goff, Philip. "Our Improbable Existence Is No Evidence for a Multiverse." *Scientific American*, January 10, 2021.

Hensen, B., et al. "Experimental Loophole-Free Violation of Bell's Inequality Using Entangled Electron Spins Separated by 1.3 km." *Nature* 526 (2015): 682–686.

Kastrup, B. "A Simple Ontology That Solves the Mind-Body Problem" (forthcoming).

Lanza, R. "The Impossibility of Being Dead." *Psychology Today*, November 11, 2020.

Lewis, G. F., and L. A. Barnes. "A Conversation on Fine Tuning." In *A Fortunate Universe: Life in a Finely Tuned Cosmos*, 1–32. Cambridge: Cambridge University Press, 2016.

Ma, X.-S., et al. "Quantum Erasure with Causally Disconnected Choice." *Proceedings of the National Academy of Sciences* 110, no. 4 (2013): 1221–1226.

Manning, A. G., et al. "Wheeler's Delayed-Choice Gedanken Experiment with a Single Atom." *Nature Physics* 11 (2015), https://doi.org/10.1038/nphys3343.

Merali, Z. "Quantum 'Spookiness' Passes Toughest Test Yet." *Nature* 525 (September 2015): 14–15.

Paulson, S. "Roger Penrose on Why Consciousness Does Not Compute." *Nautilus*, April 27, 2017.

Romero, J., et al. "Violation of Leggett Inequalities in Orbital Angular Momentum Subspaces." *New Journal of Physics* 12 (December 2010), accessed June 14, 2016, http://iopscience.iop.org/article/10.1088/1367-2630/12/12/123007.

Rosenblum, B., and F. Kuttner. "Consciousness and Quantum

Mechanics: The Connection and Analogies." *Journal of Mind and Behavior* 20, no. 3 (Summer 1999): 229–256.

Strawson, G. *Consciousness and Its Place in Nature.* Exeter, UK: Imprint Academic, 2006.

Vieira, R. "Can the Multiverse Give You an Afterlife?" *Philosophy Now* 119 (2017): 24–25.

Yoon-Ho Kim, R., et al. "A Delayed 'Choice' Quantum Eraser." *Physical Review Letter* 84, no.1 (January 3, 2000).

# About the Author

SEBASTIAN JUNGER is the *New York Times* bestselling author of *Freedom, Tribe, War, A Death in Belmont, Fire,* and *The Perfect Storm,* and codirector of the documentary film *Restrepo,* which was nominated for an Academy Award. He is also the winner of a Peabody Award and the National Magazine Award for Reporting.